P9-BZX-906

Contents

Preface

L
ibrary governance is a team sport. The team we refer to in this guide is the public library's director-board team. The library director is the coach, the board president is the team captain, and the board members are the team players.

Just like the coach of the Kansas City Chiefs or the Baltimore Ravens, the coach instructs and motivates. The team captain reinforces the instruction and motivation, adds inspiration, and models the selfless behavior needed to win. The team players bring their unique talents to the table, internalize the teachings, and practice the behaviors that allow the team to fulfill its purpose—winning!

For the library director-board team winning means fulfilling the library's *social contract* with its community, whereby the library provides materials and services that support lifelong learning, jobs, and quality of life in return for financial and other support. To win for their community, trustees must go beyond mastering the basics of managing board operations. In tandem with the director, they must go to the next level and become "players" in their community's power structure. As players they have two roles. One is helping leaders identify and achieve important community goals. The other is continuously pointing out how stakeholders, who are also the leaders' constituents, benefit from library services.

About the Book

A major premise of this strategic guide is that to be an effective team, the director, board chair, and board members must all be reading from the same page with respect to the complex issues that face libraries today.

This guide deals with five strategic issues facing virtually each of the nation's 9,214 public libraries. Two address current issues, starting with risk management. Its many facets range from meeting room policies to disaster planning. The other is balancing local values and the perceived threats to them with legal protections, especially those provided under the First Amendment.

Two other strategic issues deal with infrastructure. One is the mix of leadership and management needed by the director-board team to achieve a library's vision. The other is getting and growing the mix of funds—public and private—needed for programs and services that benefit stakeholders.

The fifth issue looks beyond the library to its community, addressing the director-board team becoming part of its community's leadership group.

Why these issues? Because our experience working with local, regional, state, and national library entities and looking through issues of *American Libraries*, *Library Journal*, *Library Administration & Management*, websites, Listservs, and so forth, shows their criticality.

The director is usually steeped in these issues by virtue of attending conferences, networking with peers, and reading the literature. Furthermore, the director is grounded in the ethics and principles that guide professional librarians. To do their job as discussed in this guide, trustees need to understand their director's point of view while also letting him or her know how the community sees these issues.

In this book, we discuss these issues in lay terms. We have written it in a brisk tone for busy trustees and directors who have only a few hours per month together to consider options and make decisions. This guide seeks to help trustees and their directors in three broad areas: (1) understanding complex issues and their local impact, (2) assessing the trustee's role in addressing those issues, and (3) reviewing experiences and best practices from other libraries. It has many uses: (1) board meeting discussions, (2) self-study, and (3) a benchmark for assessing your board's performance.

The authors are uniquely qualified to address library governance and to give their opinions of the issues. Ellen G. Miller has worked with library boards, city councils, and special district boards for over thirty-five years. Currently a member of the Kansas State Library Advisory Commission, she served as a member, then president, of the Johnson County Library in Kansas. She is the founding president of the Kansas Library Trustee Association. Nationally, she is a regional vice president of the Association of Library Trustees and Advocates (ALTA), having served earlier as second vice president. She was named to the ALA/ALTA National Advocacy Honor Roll in 2000.

Patricia H. Fisher, a public library trustee for more than ten years, served the Baltimore County Public Library in Maryland in three capacities: as library board member and president, and also as a board member of the Foundation for Baltimore County Public Library.

At the state level, she was president of the Maryland Library Association's trustee division. She currently serves on the board of the Citizens for Maryland Libraries. Nationally, she is a past president of ALTA.

Both Miller and Fisher are active authors, conference presenters, and keynote speakers. Together and separately, they have conducted numerous workshops for library trustees.

How This Book Is Organized

The issues are discussed in five chapters. And the book has a companion website (www.pfisherassociates.com/scarecrowpress/sources.html) with useful tools, such as downloadable forms, answers to chapter checkup quizzes, and more. The website address is www.pfisherassociates.com/scarecrowpress.

The chapters each begin with a quick view that summarizes the chapter. The chapters also include a definition of the issue and a discussion (both serious and lighter) of how this issue can affect directors and boards; quotes obtained from experts via interviews; sidebars with real case histories and our experiences; illustrations of forms, which can be downloaded from the book's companion website; tips, dos, and don'ts; and chapter checkup quizzes. Where applicable, selected theories from business and nonprofit experts are presented.

The guide was written with three different readers in mind. One seeks information about a specific topic, such as personnel aspects of disaster planning (chapter 1) or coping with tax increment financing (chapter 4). If you are that reader, you will find the index invaluable.

The second reader has a more general interest in, say, the dual leadership and management tasks of library boards (chapter 3). And yes, we do mean "boards." You can dip into whatever chapter piques your interest first and read the chapters in the sequence of your choice.

The third reader will go through the book sequentially. You will find that some chapters refer only briefly to a topic, such as partners or advocacy, that is treated more fully in a different chapter, as noted.

Chapter 1, "Managing Risk," discusses topics such as the many types of risk; federal, state, and local requirements; and three shields—policies, insurances, and catastrophe plans.

Chapter 2, "Local Values, the First Amendment, and Challenges," deals with the many faces of local values and investigating them, library staff and board values, and handling challenges.

Chapter 3, "Leadership and Management That Achieve Your Library's Vision," addresses topics such as why leadership matters, director-board teams, and the director-board team's three jobs—delivering benefits to your community, legitimizing a customer-benefits culture, and effective board operations.

Chapter 4, "Getting and Growing the Funding Your Library Needs," covers topics such as revenue from public and private dollars, how to make money on public funds, curbs on getting public dollars, and advocacy that protects or gets funding.

Chapter 5, "Getting on Your Community's Leadership Team," looks at the many community decision-making tables; the special case of economic development; positioning your library as a player; and learning from various-sized libraries that have become part of their power structure, such as the Chicago Public Library, serving 2.9 million, and the Aztec (New Mexico) Public Library, serving a population of about 8,000.

The home page for the companion website gives an overview and complete description of the book, and its side menu provides access to the other pages on the site. Another way to get to each of pages on the site is from the Table of Contents page. It has links to each of the chapter pages. Each chapter page starts with a summary of the book's chapter (Quick View), and it lists the downloadable forms, which can be customized. The answer key to the chapter checkup quiz is also found on each chapter page.

If at any time you want to share your experiences as a result of using this strategic guide (a) for board meeting discussions, (b) for self-study, or (c) as a benchmark for assessing your board's performance, feel free to contact one of the authors: Ellen G. Miller at www.ellenmillergroup.com or Patricia H. Fisher at www.pfisherassociates.com. We hope you keep in touch.

Acknowledgments

This guide has benefited from our friends and colleagues both in and out of libraryland, who have shared experiences and thoughts about library governance and the director-board team with us.

We are indebted to the library boards on which we served, specifically the Johnson County (Kansas) Library and its county librarian, Mona Carmack, as well as the Baltimore County Public Library and two of its directors, Charles Robinson and Jim Fish.

Wielding red pencils and asking tough questions, chapter reviewers sharpened the guide's focus. Many thanks to Gina Millsap, executive director, Topeka-Shawnee County (Kansas) Public Library; Dean Martha Hale, School of Library and Information Service, Catholic University of America; Jim Minges, director, Northeast Kansas Library System; Jim Fish, director, Baltimore County Public Library; Diana Graves, fiscal officer, Johnson County (Kansas) Library; Mary Baykan, director, Washington County (Maryland) Public Library. Special appreciation goes to Duane Johnson, former Kansas state librarian, who went extra miles by reviewing the first four chapters.

Busy trustees and directors of libraries large and small took time out for interviews. Special thanks, in alphabetical order by name of library, go to the following people:

Ames (Iowa) Public Library, director Art Weeks (formerly director of the Anchorage [Alaska] Public Library)
Arlington Heights (Illinois) Public Library, trustee G. Victor Johnson
Aztec (New Mexico) Public Library, director Leanne Hathcock
Baltimore County Public Library, director Jim Fish
Cecil County (Maryland) Public Library, director Denise Davis

Chandler (Arizona) Public Library, branch manager Brenda Brown
Chestatee (Georgia) Regional Library System, director Lyn Hopper
Chicago Public Library, commissioner Mary Dempsey
Eastern Oklahoma District Library System, executive director Marilyn Hinshaw
Farmers Branch Manske Library (Texas), trustee Diane Graifemberg
Friends of the Saint Paul (Minnesota) Public Library, president Peter Pearson
Gwinnett County (Georgia) Public Library, former director JoAnne Pinder
Indian Trails (Illinois) Public Library District, trustee Don Roalkvam
Kansas City (Missouri) Public Library, executive director Crosby Kemper III
Maywood (Illinois) Public Library District, trustee Rose Mosley
Mid-Continent (Missouri) Public Library, trustees John Laney and Brent Schondelmeyer
Morrisson-Reeves (Indiana) Library, director Carol Smyth McKey
Olathe (Kansas) Public Library, director Emily Baker
Pasadena (California) Public Library, director Jan Sanders
Plainfield-Guilford (Indiana) Public Library, director Charr Skirvin
Public Library of Charlotte and Mecklenburg County, North Carolina, senior library manager, main librarian Susan Herzog
Rochester (Michigan) Public Library, director Christine Hage
Sacramento Public Library, director Anne Marie Gold
Salt Lake City (Utah) Public Library, trustee Rosalind McGee
Seattle Public Library, city librarian Deborah L. Jacobs
Tippecanoe County (Indiana) Public Library, county librarian Jos N. Holman
Toronto Public Library, executive director Josephine Bryant
Washington County (Maryland) Public Library, director Mary Baykan
Wichita (Kansas) Public Library, director Cynthia Berner-Harris

We also interviewed executives of state and national library organizations, a local government executive, and a library consultant. They include Marilyn Gell Mason, executive director, WebJunction; Greta Southard, executive director, Public Library Association; Faye Terry, Public Library Services consultant, Indiana State Library; Sharman Smith, Mississippi state librarian; Jim Smith, Baltimore County, Maryland, executive; Jim Dodson, consultant, Braren, Mulder, German Associates, Inc.

We greatly appreciate Martín Gomez and Danielle Milam of ULC (Urban Libraries Counsel) for the opportunity to assess the needs of the trustees of their member libraries and for permission to use some of those findings in this book.

The encouragement, patience, and expertise of our editors, Martin Dillon and Patricia Zylius (copy editor), helped us break new ground in this guide through frank discussion of thorny strategic issues facing trustees and their directors.

Finally, we would like to thank our incredibly supportive and patient husbands, John Miller and Ron Fisher Sr. They made sacrifices and sometimes endured our neglect when we were busy working on this book. They bore up under dozens of—to us—riveting dinner discussions about library boards. Most important, they encouraged us to write the book we both wish we'd had when we joined our local library boards. With gratitude we thank them.

CHAPTER 1

Managing Risk

Quick View

What do potential library trustees usually hear about serving on the board? That monthly meetings last only an hour.

Reality sets in when you get a two-inch packet of materials, e-mails keep coming, and your name pops up in the local paper. Some boards are elected by voters. Others are appointed by local officials.

For full or partial governing library boards, the job has many legal and fiduciary responsibilities. For advisory library boards, the job may be mostly restricted to advocacy at city hall and advising the director. For both, chances are high that the job's much tougher than expected.

One nice surprise: the director-board team. The old saying is that the board makes policy and the director implements it. However, often the director is the maestro, orchestrating the timing and content of the review of the library's shields against risk. When the director-board team is at work, everyone contributes his or her expertise to help the library.

By design, this guide starts with the major policy area of risk management. This directly affects the library's future but is usually discussed in pieces rather than holistically. This chapter covers the following topics:

- Risk management ABCs
- The many faces of risk
- Knowing your requirements
- Stakeholder opinions
- Shield #1: policies

- Shield #2: insurances
- Shield #3: catastrophe plans
- Chapter checkup: "Congratulations, You're the New Risk Manager!"

As explained in the preface, you can check this book's linked website to download an adaptable form. Also see the website for additional sources.

Risk Management ABCs

The 2002 *Shorter Oxford English Dictionary* defines risk as "endanger, put at risk, expose to the chance of injury or loss." The 2003 *Chambers Dictionary* defines it as "hazard, danger, chance of loss or injury; the degree of probability of a loss; a person, thing or factor likely to cause loss or danger."

The issue for library boards and library directors? Moving past consideration of a few individual risks such as liability for a minor's access to the Internet, to the universe of risks. That universe has changed greatly in the past thirty years as governmental immunity to lawsuits has eroded. Libraries and their governmental peers are responsible for much more than safe sidewalks and safe kids. They also must demonstrate their accountability in using public dollars for the public's good. They need to fulfill constitutionally or other protected rights such as freedom of speech, freedom of religion, and protection of persons with disabilities.

Many eyes are watching how libraries handle risks, from federal and state regulators to library users and the media. Ignoring or minimizing the consequences of acts or omissions can jeopardize a library's quality of operations, image, or funding.

Facts and Consequences

Risks come in more flavors than salsa. Consider these library examples.

- *Director's theft.* The sentence given the library director of Homer Township (Illinois) included six months in jail, $100,000 restitution to the library, plus probation and community service. She had stolen over $157,000 from the library's petty cash account. The library board president then sought more civil suits that would bring the total to about $320,000 stolen.[1]

- *Patron behavior.* An assailant threw an egg that cut a library assistant's lip as she sat at her desk. It was another example of unruly patrons of the Lowell (Massachusetts) Public Library turning violent when corrected by employees. The ugly behavior is especially ironic given the building's multimillion-dollar improvements.[2]

- *Board controversies.* In one eventful meeting, the Gwinnett County (Georgia) Public Library board made two decisions that got national attention. First, it fired its longtime director without cause, despite one board member earlier alleging in an open letter to local newspapers that a board faction was bent on the firing. After a 3–1 vote to fire, in which the letter writer voted "no," the board cut $3,000 earmarked for more Spanish-language fiction.

  The director's firing got national library community attention, but the $3,000 cut caused a national uproar. Two weeks later, the board reversed itself. However, the firing and board reversal didn't slow down media coverage. The director's lawsuit and request for a public apology assured that the library would continue to make local and perhaps national news.[3]

- *No outside audit.* The State Board of Accounts found over $200,000 in inappropriate expenses and lack of documentation at the Indianapolis-Marion County Public Library. Purchases by the fired director, including three computers and a Palm Pilot, totaled over $27,000; none was found in the library's inventory. Another $139,000 was for undocumented credit card charges. Finally, payments made without receipts or invoices came to over $62,000. A plan to hire an outside auditing firm was launched later by the new director.[4]

Risk is a scary word, connoting events that get on TV and may scare off donors. It also stifles a major library board safeguard: candid discussion about the risks you face and how to manage them. To get things going, download figure. 1.1 and use it at an upcoming board meeting. Only a portion of the form is shown; see this book's website for the entire downloadable form.

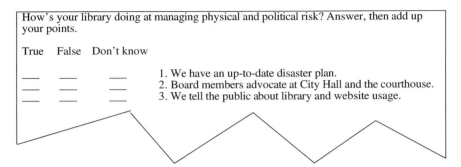

How's your library doing at managing physical and political risk? Answer, then add up your points.

True False Don't know

_____ _____ _____   1. We have an up-to-date disaster plan.
_____ _____ _____   2. Board members advocate at City Hall and the courthouse.
_____ _____ _____   3. We tell the public about library and website usage.

Figure 1.1. Risk Management Quiz

Frank discussion helps your director-board team in six ways.

1. *See the big picture.* Take the time to review risk issues and their mitigation costs together, not piecemeal. For example, does your budget include line items for D&O (directors and officers) insurance? For legal assistance? For an outside audit?

2. *Examine options.* Donor Dora may want the library to start a fee-based child care center, but what about state and local requirements, liabilities? Does a child care center fit your library vision?

3. *Minimize harmful consequences.* The library's longtime assistant director embezzled $237,000. Should the director or board president say "no comment" to the media? Or will the library cooperate in every way with authorities?

4. *Review getting stakeholder feedback.* People grouse about potholes in parking lots. They resent sullen or preoccupied staff. And they certainly have opinions about your collections and databases. Does your library provide complaint forms or an e-mail suggestion box?

5. *Discuss personal involvement.* Few library trustees expect to be criticized at board meetings, much less skewered in editorial cartoons for controversial decisions. Has your board or director team legitimized discussing personal emotions and unexpected hours spent coping with crises?

6. *Rethink orienting new trustees.* Yes, orientation lasts longer when risk management is added, but this topic helps newcomers contribute to board discussions sooner.

Discussing risk and its implications can be uncomfortable, especially when your metropolitan or local media regularly attend meetings. But doing so pays off by reducing misunderstandings later. Discussing risk holistically helps set shared expectations.

The Many Faces of Risk

Library risks have many components, starting with the persons involved. Did a particular incident involve staff or administration? An on-site user or home or office website user? Minor or adult? If a minor, with or without parental supervision?

Consider the situation. Did the occurrence involve illegal or prohibited behavior, such as accessing obscene materials or copyright infringement? Were people threatened? Were medical, police, or other professionals contacted immediately? Did staff follow policies and procedures as well as document the incident?

Assess the damage done. What or who suffered damage from the situation: people, facilities and equipment, or both? Physical or emotional injuries? Did the library keep operating or shut down? What was the impact on the library's image?

How were communications handled? How did word about the situation get out to staff, users, the media, and the community? How did the community find out about steps to rectify the situation?

Finally, review the type and amount of restitution. If monetary, was the occurrence covered by insurance? By self-insurance funds? Via short-term or long-term settlement? Or was restitution to the injured party handled through an apology or reinstated privileges?

Four-Step Program to Handle Risk

Risk management covers four areas: identification, evaluation, treatment, and implementation.

Phase 1: Identification

Identify potential exposure to tangible losses that jeopardizes a library's quality of operations, image, or funding. Table 1.1 shows some examples.

Table 1.1.   Examples of Potential Exposure to Tangible Losses

Category	Examples
• Liability	Medical and other costs caused when the bookmobile crashed into a school bus
• Property loss	Computers and collections damaged by a tornado
• Unexpected expense	Increased cost of gasoline; insurance premiums
• Revenue loss	Decreasing value of the local tax base
• Crime and fidelity loss	Poorly lit parking lots and few security measures
• Human resources loss, including employees and volunteers	Excessive turnover of IT (information technology) staff due to low salaries and poor benefits

In addition, there are the intangible items such as threats to image and credibility.

Phase 2: Evaluation

Evaluate how much will it take to hurt you in court or in the court of public opinion. One complaint every few months about cranky circulation staffers isn't a crisis, but a constant stream is. Directors can help boards get a grip through a quarterly report tracking items occurring above a certain threshold, such as insurance claims due to vehicular accidents or complaints logged onto the website.

Phase 3: Treatment

Treatment is creating a game plan to anticipate and deal with risk. What will it cost in terms of dollars, time, staff expertise, space, and image? Five typical treatment methods are as follows.

- *Loss prevention and/or reduction.* The director recommends policy changes. Once they are finalized and approved by the board, the director establishes new procedures to allow fewer occurrences of the problem. Concerning disasters, the director could recommend a biennial board review of that plan. Implementing changes, such as requiring staff to back up computer files more frequently and conducting two full-scale evacuation drills per year, is up to the director. Concerning theft prevention, the library director, working with the accountant, could create tougher procedural firewalls between money- and account-handling staff. Covering these in the director's monthly report helps the board understand the director's proactive steps.

- *Risk transfer.* This treatment shifts the financial burden from the library to another entity and can lower library costs. For example, the library joins a risk pool set up by area governmental units to get lower insurance rates and higher deductibles.
- *Risk self-help.* The library retains responsibility for making some payments via self-insurance funds for items such as stolen or disabled computers.
- *Risk avoidance.* This treatment minimizes the likelihood of complaints, grievances, and lawsuits. For example, the library's attorney, as well as managers, carefully reviews negotiated contracts and policies before coming to the board for final approval. That step ensures compliance with laws and a consistent response to, and treatment of, customers and staff.
- *Uncertainty reduction.* This final treatment of risk recognizes that local governmental units such as libraries operate in complex financial and political environments. Following their own policies and procedures is the single step most likely to reduce accidents, complaints, and lawsuits. For libraries that are city or county departments, library staff would follow the parent organization's policies for, say, competitive bidding when issuing RFPs (requests for proposals) and evaluating responses.

Phase 4: Implementation

Two time frames apply. The director identifies steps for short-term risk management possible with current FY budgets, staff, and commitments. A long-term risk management plan is included during the next cycle of operational and capital improvement budgets.[5]

These four phases help libraries assess, plan for, and carry out steps to mitigate risks. Yes, you may get tired of having risk management crop up so often on your monthly agenda. But thoughtful discussion is essential to establishing a game plan that addresses the library's major risks.

Knowing Your Requirements

Director-board team, knowing your city, county, state, and federal requirements must be a top priority. Those requirements address the board's
major roles such as owner, employer, and recipient of public funds. They fall
into two major categories: fiduciary and legal.

Fiduciary Requirements

Governing library boards are expected to oversee that funds are anticipated, received, managed, invested, and spent according to legal requirements and national accounting standards.

   In many libraries, the director manages all funds with the board's
approval. Other libraries split the work between the director and a
finance committee. Larger libraries have employees dedicated to financial management in positions ranging from a part-time bookkeeper
to a finance director with support staff. And some contract those services from their city, county, regional, other system. However your library
does it, the board must monitor the money management process and
results.

GAAP and GASB 34

Most libraries nationally use Generally Accepted Accounting Practices
(GAAP) to account for and track all funds, whether public or private.
Most libraries utilize financial controls that maximize integrity in handling, recording, and depositing funds. One aspect, cash management,
requires special consideration. Experience shows that fund and cash
handling are magnets for problems. Best practices call for firewalls that
segregate staff assignments. For example, no one employee should be
responsible for authorizing transactions, handling cash, and recording
transactions. There are exceptions, however. For example, Kansas permits an annual waiver of GAAP upon application, permitting use of cash
basis accounting.[6]

Don't confuse GAAP with General Accounting Standards Board Statement Number 34 (GASB 34), also known as the "New Reporting Model" or accrual accounting.

GASB 34 applies to all state and local government entities, including libraries. It requires putting infrastructure assets on the books, thereby depreciating them over time. Many libraries didn't do this before GASB 34; instead they just entered the price of furnishings or books in the year they were purchased. For libraries, infrastructure items include buildings, furniture, the collection, and computers and telecommunications equipment.

GASB 34 requires

- reporting on the entity's overall financial health, not just individual fund types;
- the total cost, including capital costs, of delivering services;
- general infrastructure assets such as roads and water mains;
- financial statements to be accompanied with introductory narrative analyzing the entity's financial performance.

Under GASB 34, annual reports include a Management Discussion and Analysis section. Yes, it takes staff time to write. One benefit: documenting the library's upcoming needs for capital funds to replace these depreciating infrastructure assets. When a bond issue or a mill levy increase is needed, the library has reliable information to use in making its case. The overall goal? Transparency that shows your library's accountability in managing funds to citizens, taxpayers, customers, investors, creditors, and local officials.[7]

Auditors Report to the Board, Not the Director

External audits of a library's financial management cover the entire process, from taking in a fifteen-cent fine to the bookkeeper's end-of-month closeout and required reports. The 2002 Sarbanes-Oxley Act addressed corporate governance reform in the wake of the Enron, WorldCom, and other financial scandals. Arguably its best-known provision is the requirement that chief executive officers and chief financial officers must personally certify the accuracy of financial statements and the effectiveness of internal controls; false certifications result in substantial penalties. While currently mandatory only for for-profit organizations, it is strongly recommended for the nonprofit world. Can libraries be far behind?

Under Sarbanes-Oxley, the board or its audit committee is responsible for hiring and overseeing the external auditor's work. Of organizations with an annual budget under $20 million, 67 percent had an audit committee; 57 percent met with the auditor once a year, while another 30 percent met two or three times per year.[8]

If a library's external audit reveals inadequate money-handling practices, the auditor's management letter will list them. Directors will bring that letter to the board, along with recommendations for remedies.

One related financial item: how your Friends, foundation, or other 501(c)3 support group handles its money. Their money management can reflect on the library's reputation.

Trustees, remember that the auditor must report to the board, not to the director. If by some chance your library hasn't had an external audit report in the past three years, run (don't walk) to schedule this topic at your next board meeting. Also have your director talk to your state library about regulations or statutory requirements for audits.

Getting All the Money, On Time

One pesky area: receiving all anticipated funds on time from other governmental units. A few weeks' slippage or a small percent held back gives the conduit city or county a nice windfall. And it gives your library a big problem, having to rely unexpectedly on carryovers, gift funds, or other sources to cover the shortfall. Your library made its current FY budget based on financial assumptions about both amounts received and timeliness. While some director-board teams hesitate to raise these issues with the conduit city or county agency, you likely have the law on your side. Most states' regulations specify both the number of days the conduit city or county has before transferring funds to your library and the percentage to be transferred. Sidebar 4.2 in chapter 4 shows how one lawsuit fixed delayed dollar delivery.

Escrow accounts deserve special attention. For example, a journalist's probe of Oklahoma City tax protests found that $10.6 million had been sitting dormant in an interest-bearing escrow account for twenty-five years! Beneficiaries included the Metropolitan Library System, which received $262,390.[9]

State Funding Rules

One final fiduciary risk is loss of state funding to libraries. Two situations may apply: funding cuts by the state legislature and the library not meeting standards for public libraries.

Many states provide some kind of direct state aid grants to local libraries. But the amounts often fluctuate, depending on state revenues and legislative action.

When considering state funds to local libraries, be aware of another threat: state aid cuts due to local acts of omission or commission. Virtually all states require local actions to qualify for direct state aid grants. For example, Oklahoma's *Rules and Regulations for State Aid Grants to Public Libraries* require the following:

- The library must be open to the public for at least fifteen hours a week, with two hours after 5 p.m. for cities under 2,000. For cities over 25,000, they must be open sixty hours a week with seven hours on Saturday.
- All library facilities must provide Internet access to the public.
- "Local government must continue to expend an amount for library service, i.e., operating expenditures, not less than that of the preceding fiscal year" (maintenance of local effort).[10]

For example, the Ames (Iowa) Public Library had $25,000 restored by the city for its collection budget after the library board voted for a significant

3 8539 00112 7854

budget cut. Library staff had recommended the cut, recognizing that cuts were required since the city had lost revenue as a result of the state eliminating property tax reimbursements. "However, we pointed out that the cut would mean the library was no longer in compliance with state standards," said former director Gina Millsap. In Iowa, 10 percent of an annual operating budget must be spent on collections. The library would have lost an estimated $14,000 in state funding, in addition to the local cut, for a total of $39,000.[11]

Director-board team, your state's rules help shield you from local threats. For example, when Mayor Mike wants you to cut hours or dollars, your library director can show him the math concerning potential state aid losses. A letter to him from your foundation and Friends' presidents would help, too.

Unsure about the rules concerning receiving and using funds? Line up a state library consultant to brief your board, city attorney, and city manager on applicable laws and regulations. Check to see if an attorney general opinion includes libraries either specifically or by implication.

Legal Requirements

Your library may have avoided legal hot water, but not all do. Improper use of executive session, discriminatory personnel actions, disputed access to patron records, minors' access to the Internet—the beat goes on. Minimize your library's risk by having your attorney give an annual update on applicable laws.

Federal Laws

The most important federal laws for public libraries affect privacy of users' records and minors' access to the Internet.

USA Patriot Act. The 2001 Uniting and Strengthening America by Providing Appropriate Tools Required to Intercept and Obstruct Terrorism Act (USA Patriot Act) affects all public libraries and their users as well as businesses. It greatly extended the ability of state, local, and federal law enforcement agencies to demand usage records about persons thought to be involved in terrorism or clandestine activities.

The original act enabled demands for records to be issued through an administrative subpoena called a National Security Letter (NSL) authorized under Section 505. Issued by the Federal Bureau of Investigation, they are not reviewed by a grand jury or a judge. The recipient organization, such as a library, cannot disclose that it has been served or that records were provided. Collecting personal data such as information about books checked out of the library, medical history, and goods purchased is allowed under Section 215 without evidence that the citizen is involved with terrorism. And the targeted person cannot be told his or her records are under scrutiny.

Civil rights concerns blossomed during the act's reauthorization in 2005 and 2006. Of special concern to the library community was the NSL. A 2005 American Library Association (ALA) study found that public and academic libraries had received more than 130 legally executed requests by federal, state, or local law enforcement officers since 2001. Public libraries received 63 requests; academic libraries got 74.

To notify its users, the Santa Cruz (California) Public Libraries posted signs reading, "WARNING. Although the Santa Cruz library makes every effort to protect your privacy, under the federal USA Patriot Act . . . records of the books and other materials you borrow from this library may be obtained by federal agents. That federal law prohibits library workers from informing you if federal agents have obtained records about you."

After months of delays, the USA Patriot Act's major original sections were made permanent. However, four sections, including authorizing roving wiretaps and secret searches of library, bookstore, and business records, were approved for only four years. Improvements included the following:

- Libraries, businesses, and other targets were given the legal standing to challenge "gag orders" preventing discussing the organizations. Challenges must be handled through secret court proceedings, however.
- Targets do not need to disclose their attorney's name to the government.

Shortly after the Patriot Act's 2006 reauthorization, ALA president Michael Gorman said the association will seek changes that require "the FBI to limit its search of library records to individuals who are connected to a terrorist or suspected of a crime." The ALA will also seek changes so that recipients can "pose a meaningful challenge to the 'gag' order that prevents them from disclosing the fact that they have received such an order."[12]

The Children's Internet Protection Act. Another major federal law is the Children's Internet Protection Act (CIPA). It posits that a library has a substantial and compelling interest in protecting young library users from inappropriate material on the Internet. It requires filters on all Web-connected computers if a library wants to receive federal LSTA (Library Services Technology Act) or e-rate funds.

An estimated 40 percent of the nation's libraries have complied with CIPA by installing filters. The act does allow adults to request that the filter be disconnected, but that requires customer education and staff availability. For example, Georgia's Gwinnett County Public Library handles adults' requests to unblock filters through a laptop computer in each of its fourteen branches. Employees will disable the laptop's filter. In exchange for the user's driver's license, the patron may use the laptop anywhere in the library except near the children's area. Between 1996, when filters were installed, and early 2006, there were about a half-dozen requests for the filters to be disabled.

Some libraries use a state-provided free filter service. The State Library of Kansas sponsors KanGuard, operated statewide by the Northeast Kansas Library System. Over 150 of the state's 324 public libraries participate.[13]

ADA and more. Many other federal laws affect libraries. They include the Americans with Disabilities Act (personnel, potential personnel, and customers), Equal Employment Opportunity, the Drug-Free Workplace Act, the Fair Labor Standards Act (its revised rules about who gets overtime pay, compensation time, or neither often pose problems in smaller libraries with low wages and skimpy budgets), and sexual harassment protection under the Civil Rights Act reauthorization of 1991. Is that all? No. But knowing how your library complies with these and other federal laws lets your board measure your risk.

State Laws

State laws set requirements concerning accountability for all governmental entities, including libraries. For example, "sunshine laws" seek to assure that public entities using public funds conduct their business in public. They deal with open meetings and open records. The director-board team needs to keep up on occasional changes to sunshine laws, such as adding e-mails and teleconferencing under the definition of "meeting."

Other important state laws affecting libraries involve the following issues:

- *Conflict of interest.* State language will vary concerning the types of prohibited relationships, prohibited actions, and consequences. But for the court of public opinion, adopt this down-home definition: "Don't do it if your family, friends, business acquaintances, or supporters appear to unfairly benefit." State penalties can range from loss of position and paying fines to imprisonment. Library lawyers typically advise avoiding even the appearance of a conflict of interest.
- *Apparent authority.* Library trustees have legal authority only in the aggregate, making decisions as a board. Individual members have no authority, but not everyone gets that message. Don't copy the president who committed her board to an unneeded, pricey library history. Shortly thereafter, her term ended but the board felt honor-bound to continue the author's contract.[14]
- *Filters.* For some states, CIPA didn't go far enough. After all, libraries could opt out of filtering by forfeiting federal e-rate and LSTA funds. Twenty-one states have Internet filtering laws that apply to public schools or libraries. Most require only adoption of an Internet use policy that prevents minors from accessing sexually explicit, obscene, or harmful materials. Some, such as Arizona and Minnesota, require publicly funded libraries to install filters on public access computers.[15]

Other state laws affecting libraries range from board term limits and investment of excess funds to concealed weapons. For example, the Kansas legislature enacted a licensed, concealed carry law, effective January 2007; it specifically exempts public libraries. Subsequently, the state attorney general ruled that while no signage about the prohibition is required, a library may post such signage if it desires.[16]

Local Requirements

City, county, and township ordinances and codes also affect the library. While too diverse for this guide to cover, examples likely to come to the director-board team's attention include these:

- Building codes, such as for retention ponds
- Exterior signage
- Police requirements, such as reporting abandoned children
- Fire codes, such as those regarding building occupancy
- Hazardous materials requirements for chemical or flammable items
- City and county codes, such as those for no smoking zones or easements

Directors, why remind the board how your library fulfills city and county requirements? First, it shows professional management. Second, it provides trustees with facts to use when hearing complaints at the church social about not being able to smoke outside the library anymore.

Update the media, too. While press releases about meeting local legal requirements demonstrates transparency, they may be too bland for media use. Instead, weave information about meeting or exceeding code requirements for energy efficiency into a release about the remodeled children's room. Also, post it on your website.

As a public entity, your library is in the papers and perhaps on talk radio. Positive and neutral stories can help offset the inevitable negative coverage of, say, an employee's lawsuit or the latest challenge to Harry Potter.

Stakeholder Opinions

So how does media coverage of library issues affect Dawn Doe? Apparently not much. Consider two important benchmarks of public opinion: opinion polls and referenda. Much of the time, the library wins.

A 2006 national opinion poll by the ALA of 1,000 adults showed 26 percent were extremely satisfied and 44 percent very satisfied with their public library, totaling 70 percent. In 2002, only 60 percent were very or extremely satisfied. When ranking libraries, schools, roads, parks, and libraries, 36 percent put libraries at the top of the list.

Another 2006 poll, "Long Overdue: A Fresh Look at Public Attitudes about Libraries in the 21st Century," shows similar high ratings. One thousand two hundred respondents gave an A grade to public libraries more often (45 percent) than to any other community service. Over two-thirds (71 percent) said their local library used money well. However, few were aware of libraries' difficult financial position.

Local opinion polls show results such as 82 percent of New Yorkers rating public library services as good or excellent. Citizens ranked the Johnson County (Kansas) Library as the top rated of the five county services and programs, with 90 percent selecting it.[17]

But do those high ratings carry over voters considering library referenda? Maybe. Table 1.2 shows three years of referenda results for buildings and operating budgets.

The numbers won are down from the halcyon economy in the late 1990s. For example, in 1998 both referenda passed by more than two-thirds of the vote: 82 percent for operating budgets and 71 percent for buildings. Seven years later, the percentage of votes for libraries hovered around 50 percent.[18]

How to help your referenda pass? Show how the library uses precious tax dollars to make a difference in your community through needed services, programs, and facilities. Operate those services, programs, and facilities in ways that meet or exceed legal and fiduciary requirements. Finally, use three major shields that help protect your users and library from risk: policies, insurance, and catastrophe plans.

Table 1.2.   Referenda Results for Public Libraries, 2003–2005

	2003				2004				2005			
Type	Won		Lost		Won		Lost		Won		Lost	
	N	(%)	N	(%)	N	(%)	N	(%)	N	(%)	N	(%)
Buildings	45	(76)	14	(24)	34	(69)	15	(31)	25	(52)	23	(48)
Operating budgets*	70	(83)	14	(17)	46	(70)	20	(30)	33	(57)	25	(43)

*Excludes New York, which by state law could potentially have 175/year

Shield #1: Policies

Policies are like chain saws or airplanes; they can be useful or dangerous. To help, policies must cover key areas and be kept up-to-date. Who's in charge of that process? Directors.

This Just In: Policies Start with Directors

The old cliché says boards make policy, directors implement it. But that's too simple. A director's job includes guiding your board in many aspects of policymaking. Directors, only you think about libraries 24/7/365. Trustees have many other topics on their minds, ranging from other volunteer commitments to details like jobs and family. Only you can effectively orchestrate crucial policy areas such as these:

- *The sequence needed*—for example, recommending a higher age at which minors can get their own library card before requiring a library card to use Internet workstations
- *Knowledge level*—for example, scheduling an IT expert to discuss trends in wireless connectivity or a peer library's development director to discuss tips about starting a library foundation
- *Timing*—for example, completing your collection development policy review before budget discussions start
- *Content*—for example, providing recommendations about parents' ability to see what their minor children have checked out. Do be sure to address confidentiality issues.

Trustees, here's where "Homework Is Us!" truly applies. Don't break your director's heart by tearing open your board packet as discussion starts on Policy 121, gifts of library materials. Instead, review that packet ahead of time. For a point of comparison, check out the gift policy posted on a peer library's website.

One important distinction: policy versus practice. It's up to the director and staff to create and implement procedures that carry out those revised policies.

In summary, one truly essential director task is managing the process of creating, reviewing, and updating policies. The counterpart trustee task is thoughtful, informed policy discussions at board meetings. When both jobs are carried out, the cliché becomes true: The board has approved policy that the director implements.

Your Policies: Rock Solid or Swiss Cheese?

Library policies and bylaws are part of your legal framework. They are the first place attorneys on both sides will go in the event of a grievance or lawsuit. The media will want to see them when the Southside Skinheads are refused use of your meeting room—and when they are permitted to use it!

Questioners will ask if the policies state criteria, procedures, and ways to appeal decisions. What about the type and frequency of staff training? What kind of paper trail is created, and how long is it kept? Does the policy reflect recent changes in laws and regulations?

If either the policy or supporting procedures are deficient, better get the library's checkbook out. You'll likely spend money on items such as your attorney's fees and perhaps specialist attorney fees to conduct an outside inquiry. Costs for staff overtime to find and prepare the paper trail mount up. It's possible you'll need public relations assistance or damage control. Last and not least, remember the possible actual and punitive damages paid to the victim.

Policies cut both ways. Dangerous when poorly maintained and implemented, they are also one of your best barriers against risk when staff apply them consistently and quickly.

Four Must-Have Policies

Libraries have dozens or even hundreds of policies. But not all are equal when it comes to risk management. Trustees, thumb through your library's policy manual or cruise your website. Check out the topics, which can range from "abusive language" to "youth services." Of the dozens of policies, four areas deserve special attention:

- Minors
- Customer relations
- Collection development
- Meeting rooms

Why these four? Because they address major parts of the implied social contract between the library and its funders, especially taxpayers. In return for the latter's dollars, the library provides resources, facilities, and services that improve the community.

The library's part of the social contract with funders has three main parts. *Criteria* define what resources, facilities, and services are selected. *Access* addresses how taxpayers and other stakeholders get to those resources, facilities, and services. *Values* cover stakeholders' treatment by staff and management when using, or seeking to use, those resources, facilities, and services.

Policies express the way your library will carry out its part of that social contract. Look at peer libraries' policies; many are available on their websites. Just Google a library's name. Make sure your policies cite relevant state or other laws. Have your attorney review the draft, making sure it meets any statutory or regulatory requirements. Allow ample time for board discussion, perhaps extending over two or three meetings.

By design, some policies contain both policy language (why) and a description of important procedures (how). Why? To help the board and employees see how customers will be affected.

Well-written, up-to-date library policies set expectations for all parties— patrons, staff, managers, stakeholders, the media. Standardizing those expectations helps in having fewer complaints, grievances, and lawsuits.[19]

Minors

Nothing gets your library on your paper's front page faster than being accused of not protecting kids. Library policies concerning children reflect state and federal statutes, as well as local concerns. Those policies and their supporting procedures provide staff with operational guidance about, say, an unattended six-year-old.

Pornography. Arguably the hottest issue that public libraries face, controversy starts with confusing definitions. Many consider *pornography* as synonymous with *obscenity*. But only three types of materials are illegal: child pornography, materials found to be—not alleged to be—obscene, and that which is harmful to minors.

Relevant library policies need to clearly state what's permitted and what's not and cite specific state and federal laws. For example, a library's policy concerning use of its computer workstations might state these rules:

- Patrons shall not access or exhibit obscene material (cite state statute).
- Patrons shall not possess an image in which a real child under X years is shown or heard engaging in sexually explicit conduct with the intent to arouse or satisfy the sexual desires or appeal to the prurient interest of the offender, the child, or another person (cite state statute).

For more about pornography and the three illegal types of materials— child pornography, items found to be obscene, and materials harmful to minors—see chapter 2.

Unattended child. Often kids are dropped off at the library. Not only is babysitting a very poor use of staff time, it also carries liabilities concerning the child's welfare. Policies concerning unattended children typically include statements such as these:

- Parents and others responsible for children may not leave a child age X and under unattended in any library area.

- Parents are responsible for the child's behavior and safety.
- Staff will not agree to a request to "keep an eye on" a child and will not allow a parent to order the child to stay in the library alone.
- When a child is found to be unattended, staff will try to contact the parent.
- If it's felt that the child's safety or well-being is jeopardized, staff will call the police.

Closing time presents special problems. The policy needs to clearly state that an unattended child under the age of X left at the library may, after efforts have been made to telephone a parent or other appropriate person, be treated as abandoned and in need of care. This designation then permits a request to police to take charge.

Filters. As noted earlier in this section, CIPA requires public libraries getting e-rate discounts or applying for LSTA funds to use filters on all computers accessing the Internet. These policies usually include items such as the following:

- Citation of CIPA and other relevant federal laws, along with any state or local laws
- A declaration that minors will have only filtered access to the Internet
- A statement that adults may request, and receive, disabling of those filters
- A definition of *minor*, such as individuals who are under seventeen years of age
- A safety plan including technology measures, disabling filters for adults, and expectation that library computers will be used only in lawful ways
- Loss of privileges for violators

In loco parentis. It means "in the place of the parent." Many libraries have a statement that they will not act in loco parentis; it is up to the parent to guide his or her child. The concept cuts to the critical issue of who is responsible for a minor's behavior—the library or the parent?

Consider Internet access. Depending on state law or whether the library elected to comply with CIPA, some libraries permit a parent or guardian to authorize in writing that the minor may use the Internet without adult supervision. For example, Delaware state law permits a minor's parent or guardian to specify the level of Internet access that a minor may have.

Statements concerning who's responsible for a minor's behavior may appear in both the values section of the strategic plan and in the policies.

For example, the sixth value statement of the Tippecanoe County (Indiana) Public Library's strategic plan says, "Parental responsibility. We expect parents to guide and supervise their children's use of library collections, services and programs. TCPL's board and staff do not serve *in loco parentis*, as a substitute for parents."[20]

Typical in loco parentis policy statements include these:

- It is the parents—and only the parents—who may restrict their children—and only their children—from access to library materials and services.
- When a guardian or parent signs a library card application for a child under age X, he or she agrees to responsibility for all materials checked out on the card and for the child's selection of materials.

Customer Behavior

Another major policy area is user behavior. This set of policies sets expectations by both library users and staff for allowable actions. A patron code of behavior would likely contain sections on these topics:

- *Purpose*—to protect the majority of library users from inappropriate behavior by others
- *Repercussions*—actions that could be taken by the library when a patron is asked to cease the prohibited behavior but refuses to do so
- *Staff actions*—the employee in charge may ask for assistance from a supervisor or from the local police department
- *Appeal*—steps that the disruptive patron may take to appeal the repercussions

Definitions of disruptive behavior might include failing to comply with library regulations or staff instruction; using library computers to display inappropriate material; carrying weapons; dangerous or unruly behavior disruptive to other users, staff, or oneself; and using cell phones in prohibited areas.

Staff training and drills help prepare for handling events ranging from drippy sandwiches eaten at computers to the cursing patron who refuses to quiet down.

Including police or other outreach officers assigned to the library helps when drafting your customer behavior policy and procedures. For example, each Baltimore County police precinct has a community outreach unit; its staff offer assistance and workshops concerning security-related issues. When reporting an emergency via 911, Baltimore County Public Library staff are told that they'll get the quickest response when the incident is reported to the dispatcher as being "in progress."[21]

Collection Development

Library collections, like fur coats and movie ratings, attract controversy. No matter what books, videos, or databases your library acquires or ignores, someone will disagree. Your best safeguard? Regular review of your collection development policy.

Start by making sure it links with outcomes and goals in your strategic plan. Cover how evaluation, weeding, and retention will be handled. Spell out that a mix of traditional and electronic materials and databases will be procured.

Typical collection development policy sections include these issues:

- What the library does not acquire, such as extensive genealogy materials due to cooperative arrangements with area repositories.
- Subject-by-subject review of current collection status at each branch, including what's needed to be purchased due to existing materials being outdated or existing materials not available in languages spoken by new users.
- Other resources and repositories often utilized, such as governmental agencies, historical societies, and county libraries.[22]

Trustees, your collection policy's importance cannot be overstated. It links your strategic plan to materials on shelves. Staff use it in selection, evaluation, and weeding. And when materials challenges arise, as discussed in chapter 2, it's the first place lawyers and the media will go.

Meeting Rooms

Meeting room usage is another policy lightning rod. For example, Chesterfield County, Virginia, permitted the white-supremacist World Church of the Creator, based in Peoria, Illinois, to hold a meeting in the Chester Library. Over 100 police officers guarded the library; over 500 people, mostly African Americans, attended. There were no arrests. Afterward, the library changed its policy to require an advance deposit for any needed security staff.[23]

Library policies on meeting rooms often include statements that cover the following:

- Allowed purposes, such as educational, cultural, intellectual, recreational, or charitable activities
- Allowed users, such as government or nonprofit entities
- Open access assuring that the public may attend
- Room usage, which does not constitute the library's endorsement of the group or the meeting's content

Are these the only four policies that boards need to review? Of course not. But regular review of these controversial topics should help the director-board team and staff set customer expectations. In addition to up-to-date policies, two other important shields against risk are insurances and disaster plans.

Shield #2: Insurances

Insurances form the second cornerstone of a library's risk management plan. Their appeal includes set coverage in return for a set fee.

Directors, insurances are indeed part of your turf. However, an annual board briefing will help review facts while confirming that you're getting the best coverage for the lowest price. For example, when the Gwinnett (Georgia) County Library bids insurance, it uses the county's risk manager as an advisor. A former library business manager provides consulting assistance on fees and helps analyze bids.[24]

Four Insurances

Insurance for libraries is a complex topic, affected by differing state requirements. Other factors include being a stand-alone entity or part of a city or county; size of deductibles, typically higher for larger libraries; being part of a multientity pool; and inclusion of speedy recovery services in an emergency. Libraries normally use four insurances.

Comprehensive general liability. This coverage addresses costs incurred in the course of lawsuits alleging bodily injury or property damage legal liability. It can provide for items such as "no fault" medical insurance, providing payment to the library for medical bills paid for those injured on the premises. It usually has dollar limits per person and per accident.

Umbrella liability. It covers your library above and beyond your other insurance coverages.

Property. A broader category is "all risk," which covers all items not specifically excluded by the policy. One type, "named peril," lists items such as fire, lightning, and explosions.

Directors and officers (also known as errors and omissions). It covers what your liability policies don't. It addresses the personal liability of directors (trustees) and officers for actions taken as board members, including costs to defend them. Exclusions may include libel and slander, fines and penalties imposed by courts, bodily injury and property damage claims, pollution, a deliberate act of dishonesty, and suits by one board member against another. In addition, some trustees' personal homeowner policies address such suits.

Insurance Pools

Some public libraries are insured through their parent city or county, which may in turn be part of an even larger insurance pool. Items to consider concerning insurance pools include these:

- *Your city's or county's deductible.* What is it? Does it drop or increase after a certain number of events? Does the numbering of events restart each fiscal year?
- *Reporting an event.* Be sure you know which city or county administrator to contact. Sometimes events estimated to come under the parent entity's deductible aren't reported, meaning the city or county or library must eat the cost.
- *Needed steps.* Know what your pool administrator wants in the way of documentation such as videos; printouts of withdrawn materials, furniture, and equipment; and invoices related to cleanup and repair.
- *Dealing with an adjuster.* Getting additional restoration or repair may require approval by the insurance adjuster. Know whether you need to send hard copies or e-mails, including documentation about payments made or encumbered.
- *Reimbursement process.* The pool entity that deals with the insurance company gets a check, then reimburses the library. If your city or county is part of a larger insurance pool, it could take weeks or even months before you see dollars.
- *Local building code.* Often an insurance rider requires that a damaged facility be brought up the to current building code. Deficiencies need to be documented by a qualified professional such as an architect. Bringing your facility up to code takes not only money but additional time. To avoid unrealistic promises to library users and the media about reopening, find out how long the entire code update process might take. Eager users need to be told it's likely to take months, not weeks.

Check Your Coverage

Directors, periodically update your board on your insurance coverage, especially concerning the following:

- *Building or structures.* Whether your library owns or rents, make sure you have coverage that pays for reconstruction, recovery, and repairs. This includes walls, floors, ceilings, HVAC, and other equipment.

- *Contents.* Typically this means equipment, furniture, shelving, carpets, and so on. Make sure you keep your values up-to-date to get replacement value, not original purchase value. It does not include records, files, documents, and papers.
- *Valuable papers.* Don't get fooled by the word *papers.* This clause covers all the information sources in your library—books, magazines, documents, archives, microfiche, and so on. Its value is based on your information inventory as determined from your up-to-date catalog plus any cataloging backlogs. Experts advise updating your inventory's replacement value every three years. Do include minutes, leases, and other administrative records.

  Expect to insure for only one-third of the inventory's value; insuring for more would involve huge premiums and likely attract few or no insurers.
- *Computers and telecommunications.* These riders usually cover obtaining temporary space as well as replacement costs for all items involving a computer. Data recovery is not usually included, however.
- *Equipment checks or audits, cleaning, drying, and recertification included.* Usually the goal is functional replacement meaning you might get a newer workstation if your older one is no longer sold. Time and financial limits apply; for example, expenses and rentals might last for only sixty days.
- *Temporary facilities due to business interruption.* This rider covers renting space, equipment, phones, and furnishings as well as hiring temporary staff. In some cases, it pays for unemployment insurance. Reconstructing paper documents and files is usually included, but not computer files. Usually this clause lasts for twelve months.[25]
- *A professional assessment of your insurances.* Director-board team, consider getting this done. Not only may authorizing an insurance audit provide an outsider's opinion, but also it may be a good time to discuss the pros and cons of starting or increasing

self-insurance arrangements. Some organizations self-insure by themselves; others are part of a pool. For all, the typical method is annual allocation of funds so that a growing amount is available when need occurs.

Discussing your insurance audit also sets the stage for reviewing your plans to address this guide's third and final major risk topic: disasters and emergencies.

Shield #3: Catastrophe Plans

The 2005 hurricane season was a wake-up call for libraries. The size and longevity of Katrina's and Rita's devastation of the Gulf Coast area were unprecedented. Katrina hit Louisiana, Mississippi, and Alabama; a month later Rita struck the Louisiana-Texas border.

2005 Hurricanes Meant New Priorities

Louisiana saw twenty-nine public libraries totally destroyed with another thirty-five losing their collections. In Mississippi, eleven public libraries were totally or partially destroyed; two public libraries were lost in Alabama. Available Mississippi cost estimates show $24 million for facilities damage, with another $15 million for collections and equipment. In Louisiana, the cost is estimated to be $63 million.

People First, Documentation Second

Libraries in the three states faced huge jobs, all needing to be done simultaneously. First came people issues such as finding and helping their own employees. For those libraries still operating, "people" issues aside from their own staff included the following tasks:

- Helping locate missing friends and family through website links to hurricane information sites and "missing persons" pages.

- Assisting in filling out and filing Federal Emergency Management Agency (FEMA) forms for help. Available public computers were often swamped, requiring reservation systems.
- Providing extra family and youth services, from issuing temporary cards to nonresidents to providing in-library counseling.
- Helping the public keep up on hurricane news by placing TVs in public rooms.
- Housing rescue and humanitarian organizations.

In addition to the people issues, libraries also documented damaged records, equipment, collections, and so on. They estimated how much insurance FEMA and others might pay—and when; most Mississippi libraries carried insurance on building contents, and their parent governments insured the building. One critical task: working with the local FEMA agent to get permission for virtually everything—cleaning up, moving materials, treating mold, getting a building permit, and much more.

Shortly after the hurricanes hit, state library websites in Mississippi, Louisiana, Florida, and Alabama offered information and advice to their libraries. Solinet, Inc., serving libraries in the southeastern United States, offered assistance such as nonmonetary donations, volunteers, recovery funding, and temporary housing. It also asked for help from libraries outside the affected areas.

Nationally, the ALA opened a Hurricane Katrina website. Hundreds of libraries signed up for the Adopt a Library program. Over $300,000 was collected.

In June 2006, three groups donated $17.7 million to help libraries hit by Katrina and Rita. The Bill and Melinda Gates Foundation provided $12.2 million, the Bush-Clinton Katrina Fund gave $5 million, and the Institute for Museum and Library Services provided $500,000.[26]

Advice from Mississippi's State Librarian

Nine months after Katrina, Mississippi state librarian Sharman Smith identified key factors other libraries would likely confront.

Expect substantial delays and costs in reopening a damaged library. Scarcity of materials and workers; lack of communications; and the complexities of dealing with multiple entities such as FEMA, insurance companies, and governing authorities can substantially impact recovery efforts. Smith said,

> Our affected public libraries are in catch 22 situations. They have filed for insurance and FEMA, but FEMA regulations require that insurance claims are settled before FEMA funds are distributed. Since many insurance claims are being denied or allowable reimbursements drastically reduced, litigation/arbitration to resolve the insurance issues could take years.
>
> In addition, new building requirements are being issued by FEMA which will significantly impact any renovation or new construction. For instance, the Pascagoula Library was told the building will have to be elevated several feet OR a series of retaining structures be built around the building. Also, libraries cannot count on funding from local sources because the local tax base in many of these communities is gone. In some of our communities as much as 95 percent of the local tax base has evaporated.

Predisaster relationships are critical. These include who has emergency authority, and getting them to act quickly; knowing what steps need to be taken in-house and in the community; and whom to count on.

Concentrate on the top priorities. Start by communicating with staff and governing authorities. Other tasks include accessing the library and assessing the situation, communicating with disaster recovery service providers, and identifying resources you can control.

Take charge. The first item? Be patient. Everything will take longer than expected, in part due to the immensity of the situation and also because others are dealing with their own unexpected situations. Be a leader, speaking with authority, delegating, saying "yes" and "no" a lot—this isn't a time for consensual decision making.

Reestablish a library presence quickly. "Whether it's in a loaned meeting room or trailer, get some library services going as fast as possible,"

Smith concluded."Your community and evacuees from other areas need your library to help find loved ones, provide information and be a point of semi-normalcy in their lives."[27]

Time taken to carefully create or review your library's disaster plans will save lives, resources, and money. It will also demonstrate to all staff your director-board team's commitment to serving the community.

Emergency versus Disaster Plans

The unprecedented geographic size and amount of devastation caused by the 2005 hurricanes show the need for two types of catastrophe plans for a library: emergency and disaster. As defined here, "emergency" plans address serious daily disruptions affecting health, safety, or property. Typically they affect only a few people in one facility. Examples include arson or a patron heart attack.

In contrast, "disaster" plans cover events that likely affect health, safety, and property on a huge financial or geographic scale. Their consequences may include closing one or more libraries for days or weeks before reopening. Examples include tornados, hurricanes, and terrorist actions.

Libraries need both emergency and disaster plans. For information about emergency planning, see this book's website, and click "Additional Sources." The rest of this section addresses disaster plans, from first discussions to the first simulation drill.

Disaster Planning Process

The good news? The library literature and websites have dozens of aids concerning disaster planning. You don't have to invent anything.[28]

The bad news? It takes many hours and steps to use those aids and do disaster planning right.

Directors, help your board understand the complexity of preparing and maintaining an up-to-date disaster plan. Some trustees may think all it takes is a template that staff fill out, plus an occasional drill. Since trustees will undoubtedly be contacted by the media during a disaster, review these four aspects of a disaster plan with them.

1. *Mitigation and prevention.* This means putting scarce library resources—money, staff, space—into identifying and minimizing disaster risks. Amend the operational budget to include funds for tools and technology, such as detectors. Estimate the staff time needed to research and write up a disaster plan. Add in the director-board team's time to authorize the planning process, training staff, and carrying out disaster simulations. Do include required space for records, tool storage, and staff offices.

2. *Planning.* The library can't do it alone. It takes the right mix of library, county, city, and perhaps other authorities to prepare and implement your disaster plan. Since the 9/11 terrorist attacks, several federal laws require local government, often counties, to prepare plans to participate in the nation's Integrated Emergency Management System. Most states also have a similar requirement. Discuss your county's local emergency operations plan and the library's role with its county coordinator.[29]

3. *Response.* Be sure to provide step-by-step instructions to managers and staff alike about who does what in given circumstances. The three main types of responses are notification and building evacuation; assessing the situation and damage once the disaster has occurred; and rescuing and recovering collections, computers, and facilities.

4. *Recovery.* Restoring all elements—facilities, utilities, collections, and so on—to operable mode takes the cooperation of several players. Police, city or county authorities, and insurers are just the major entities you'll work with.

Director-board team, don't skimp when discussing these concepts and costs. They inform your authorizing work when you start sketching out four must-have sections of your plan.

Four Key Components

Your disaster plan may be long or short, but its essential sections address the response team, stakeholder communications, utilizing employees' legal protections, and contacting your insurance representatives.

Form a library disaster response team. It would likely include the director or assistant director along with managers of technical services, collections, and facilities. One person would be designated as spokesperson, typically the library director or public relations person. Get the team's 24/7 contact information such as home, work, and cell phones; also e-mail, website, and physical addresses. One warning: Don't rely exclusively on cell phones. Damaged towers and overloaded networks rendered them unreliable in disasters ranging from the 9/11 terrorist attacks to hurricanes.

Set up a system of stakeholder communications. Start by identifying the library's stakeholders, then move to communications methods and frequency. List methods to let the public know if the library is open, where, and what days and hours. Of special importance: the status of computers to check on the safety and whereabouts of family and friends.

Decide how to communicate with staff and library managers. They need not only to hear the latest but also to be able to report problems, ideas, and offers of help.

Get 24/7 contact lists for your director-board team; they'll need to know facts about the emergency and steps being taken. To avoid confusion by possibly conflicting statements, they also need to be reminded who the spokesperson is.

Find ways to contact vendors. They will need directions about handling orders and deliveries. It may take several days or even weeks to sort that out. Typically this is handled by the appropriate library unit, such as technical processing or facilities.

Utilize employees' legal protections. While staff training helps them respond to an emergency, the fact is that individual behavior will vary. Some may flee the scene. Others may rush to help victims, thereby risking lawsuits later due to their actions or the consequences of them.

Some states have Good Samaritan laws addressing personal liability despite good intentions. In Maryland, staff are protected from civil damage liability by the Emergency Medical Care Law provided that the action or omission is not one of gross negligence. Providing this information in your staff guides as well as during training will help employees understand the facts about their personal risk and legal protections.[30]

Contact your insurance experts. These persons may be insurance agents or city or county employees. Review relevant disaster coverage, for the library itself and perhaps for your city or county, if it owns a building that houses library functions such as technical services. For example, does coverage include all computers, software, and telecommunications? Artworks? Rare books and items? Exhibits? Does it include rent for a temporary facility? What about contracted services to dry, clean, or repair?

With these four sections sketched out, it's time for putting the disaster plan on an upcoming board agenda. Discussion may span two or three board meetings; then it's time to write the plan.

Writing Up Your Disaster Plan

Most of the library sources noted earlier advise writing a plan with these core sections.

1. *Cover sheets.* List 24/7 contact information for agencies such as police, hazmat (hazardous materials) responders, the fire department, insurers, utilities, the media, key library personnel, and others such as locksmiths and videographers and photographers. This section also needs to state where copies of the plan, both hardcopy and electronic, are located. Include who'll supervise taking photos and videos of damage.
2. *Priorities for salvaging computers, collections, and so on.* When you have only hours to enter the library before access is shut down, prioritized lists will be essential. Set collection priorities that range from the irreplaceable (such as rare local histories or art works) to that which will be discarded or replaced anyway (such as old issues of *National Geographic*).

Setting priorities for computers, telecommunications, and automated services usually starts with in-house IT staff. City or county office IT personnel may be required to participate. Priorities should cover servers, internal databases, local area networks, Internet connections and resources, online public catalog and circulation systems, and the library's website.

3. *Emergency instructions.* Staff need to know the sequence of steps to take, such as the following:

Step 1. Call 911 or the fire department.
Step 2. Evacuate the building.
Step 3. Shut off heating and air conditioning.
Step 4. Notify designated staff and managers, including the spokesperson.
Step 5. The spokesperson notifies the media to reach the public. The community needs to know ASAP what happened, how it's being handled, whether or not they can use the facility, and how they can stay updated.

4. *Preparing to return to the library.* This section of your disaster plan covers a huge piece of territory. It addresses interim library services. It covers steps directors and staff need to take before going back into the damaged building. Providing interim services might require renting and equipping a temporary library or administrative offices—but who'll pay for it? The insurers? The insurance pool? The city or county?

Anticipating your return to the damaged facility, find out who must authorize the return: a county official, an insurance expert, or the police? Other aspects of that return include having procured required emergency equipment and supplies on hand, such as hard hats and upgraded first-aid kits.

5. *Returning to the library and cleaning up.* This section addresses required library coordination with city or county offices, police and fire departments, IT experts, and insurers before reentering

the library. Once the building is declared safe to go inside, walk through. Take videos and copious notes. Use your disaster planning checklists. For example, what construction and cleaning steps are needed? How does the library dispose safely of debris and hazardous materials?

6. *Restoring the library and collections.* Important topics include selecting and using drying methods; packing and labeling materials; and dealing with mold, insects, and pests. Once the building is rebuilt and cleaned and dry, refurnish it. Wait until all materials are completely dry before reshelving. Do make sure HVAC units are working; check for mold randomly for at least the first month.

7. *Addressing stress.* This section of your plan recognizes that emergencies breed stress. Symptoms can vary from crying and immobility to refusal to take breaks or let others help. Let managers and personnel know ahead of time the aids that are available

Sidebar 1.1. Stress and the Oklahoma City Bombing

When the McMurrah Federal Building was bombed in 1995, the closest library was just one-half block away. The Oklahoma City downtown library, part of the Metropolitan Library System, sustained immense damage to the facility and its collections. Three weeks before his death in 2006, former director Lee Brawner discussed the bombing's impact on staff. Excerpts follow:

- Our plan sort of worked, but we didn't anticipate a widespread geographic disaster affecting a 12-block area and over 500 buildings. Our plan anticipated fire and water damage, but it was overwhelmed by events.
- We had done drills in all 15 buildings. We had arranged for two emergency operational centers, but it turned out they were not technically sophisticated enough concerning computers, cabling and back-up power.
- Our plans didn't address psychological damage for either our staff or their families. But we had staff breaking down in tears, including me when I saw the children's area that was awaiting a story hour visit from the nursery housed in McMurrah. So many of those children died.
- I contacted a leading trauma psychologist who met with all the staff. He told them what to expect. This kind of session should be held immediately, ideally the next day after the disaster.
- Our medical coverage covered both group and individual counseling. Far more females participated initially, but eventually many of the men did, too. For some, the trauma lasted for three to four years.
- As a crime scene, we had to get FBI screenings and approval to get back in the building, cover up electronic gear and get personal belongings.
- Due to the fire, we had to get the fire marshal's OK to get back in. I had to remember that it was NOT our building during that period.[31]

to them, such as stress counselors, flexible hours, and emergency leave—and how much is covered by their medical insurance. As Lee Brawner states in sidebar 1.1, "We had staff breaking down in tears, including me when I saw the children's area that was awaiting a story hour visit from the nursery housed in McMurrah [Federal Building]."[32]

Director-board teams, your disaster plan may be short or extensive. Whatever its size, including all the above sections will help you, your managers, and staff deal more effectively with people, collections, and facilities. In addition, it will give your team the needed assurance that all players are as prepared as possible for saving lives and restoring library service.

The final step? Conducting simulation drills at least annually. Do include the appropriate city or county emergency staff in their design and execution. Just like military boot camp, every practice will help reduce personal and property damage in a real-life event.

The Final Word

Risk to public libraries comes in many shapes, from financial to legal to physical damage. Managing risk is a strategic governance task requiring three major shields: up-to-date library policies, adequate insurance coverage, and a comprehensive disaster plan.

Having your risk management shields in place permits the director-board team to turn to another strategic area: maintaining the implied social contract between funders, especially taxpayers, and the library. Chapter 2 addresses ties that bind and strain that social contract.

CHAPTER CHECKUP:
"CONGRATULATIONS, YOU'RE THE NEW RISK MANAGER!"

You've just been named risk manager for your library. You're scheduled to give a board briefing on the library's major risks in three weeks.

```
 ┌─────────────────────────────────────────────────────────────────────────┐
     1. Jot down the three current library risks that worry you most.

     _____  _____  _____

     2. Put these steps concerning disaster planning in the correct sequence (for
 answers, see this book's website).
     Sequence
     _____    Announce the committee's charge to the media.
     _____    Contract for off-site emergency computer and IT space.

     *More . . .*

     3. List three points that your director-board team must understand about the
 library's risks:
     1.)_____

     *More . . .*
```

Figure 1.2.   Chapter Checkup on Risk Management

Download this form, "Chapter Checkup on Risk Management," which is illustrated in figure 1.2, to get going (see the website for answers). Now you're ready for your board presentation.

Notes

1. "Illinois Librarian Sentenced," *American Libraries* 36, no. 2 (February 2005): 21.

2. Leonard Kniffel, "Maybe We *Should* Shush," *American Libraries* 35, no. 1 (January 2004): 46.

3. "Gwinnett County Board Fires Director," *American Libraries* 37, no. 7 (August 2006): 11–12.

4. "Indianapolis Library Faces Auditors, Lawsuit," *American Libraries* 35, no. 10 (October 2004): 18.

5. Based on items including Nicholas Griefer, "Risk Management: A Primer for Finance officers and Public Managers," *Government Finance Review* 17, no. 3 (June 2001): 31–37; Kevin Harper, "Saving Dollars by Managing Risk," *The American City & County* 113, no. 4 (April, 1998): 8; *Limiting Small Town Liability: A Risk Management Primer for Small Town Leaders* (Washington, DC: National Center for Small Communities, 2002), 19–22.

6. Based on items including G. Stevenson Smith, *Accounting for Libraries and Other Not-for-Profit Organizations*, 2nd ed. (Chicago: ALA Editions, 1999);

G. Stevenson Smith, *Managerial Accounting for Libraries and Other Not-for-Profit Organizations*, 2nd ed. (Chicago: ALA Editions, 2002). See also http://da.state.ks.us/ar/muniserv/GaapWaiverProcedures.htm.

7. Thomas J. Hennen Jr., "Do you Know the Real Value of your Library?" *Library Journal* 126, no. 11 (June 15, 2001): 48–50.

8. *National Board Governance Survey for Not-for-Profit Organizations* (Chicago: Grant Thornton LLP, 2005).

9. Alex Sinclair, "Windfall for OK Schools, Libraries," *School Library Journal* 50, no. 9 (September 2004): 22.

10. *Rules and Regulations for State Aid Grants to Public Libraries*. Adopted by ODL Board on April 1, 1999, www.odl.state.ok.us/servlibs/l-files/stateaid.htm; Gina Millsap, former director of the Ames (Iowa) Public Library, e-mail to authors, August 11, 2006.

11. *Rules and Regulations*; Millsap, e-mail to authors.

12. Based on items including the American Library Association's *The State of America's Libraries: Executive Summary* released April 3, 2006, www.ala.org/ala/pressreleases2006/march2006/statesummary.htm; Barton Gellman, "Americans Under Scrutiny," *Washington Post*, November 6, 2005; "ALA President Michael Gorman Responds to House Passage of PATRIOT Act Reauthorization Bill," ALA press release, July 3, 2006, American Library Association, 2006, www.ala.org/ala/pressreleases2006/march2006/PATRIOTReauthsenate.htm.

13. Based on items including Amy Lisewski Lavell, "In the Name of In(ternet)decency," *Public Libraries* 43, no. 6 (November/December 2004): 353–59; John Carlo Bertot, Charles R. McClure, and Paul T. Jaeger, *Public Libraries and the Internet 2004: Survey Results and Findings* (Tallahassee: Florida State University, 2005), 22; JoAnne Pinder, former director, Gwinnett County (Georgia) Library, e-mail to authors, October 3, 2006.

14. Statement made to author Ellen Miller, during a trustee workshop; name and state preserved to protect anonymity.

15. *Children and the Internet: Laws Relating to Filtering, Blocking and Usage Policies in Schools and Libraries*, National Conference of State Legislatures, January 20, 2006, www.ncsl.org/programs/lis/CIP/filterlaws.htm.

16. Marc Galbraith, "Concealed Carry and Kansas Libraries," Law for Librarians Blog, http://lawforlibrarians.blogspot.com.

17. Based on items including @ *Your Library: Attitudes towards Public Libraries Survey 2006*, American Library Association; www.ala.org/ala/ors/reports/2006KRC Report.pdf; "Long Overdue: A Fresh Look at Public and Leadership Attitudes about

Libraries in the 21st Century," Americans for Libraries Council, 2006, www.lff.org/long_overdue061306.html; Francine Fialkoff, "Advocating Friends," *Library Journal* 128, no. 1 (January 2003): 78; "2005 Citizen Survey," www.jocogov.org, search for the exact phrase "2005 citizens survey," then select the second item, "Key Documents and Reports," then select "2005 Citizen Survey" from "County Documents and Reports."

18. Anne Marie Gold, "By the People," *Library Journal* 131, no. 5 (March 15, 2006): 40–44.

19. Based on items including Johnson County (Kansas) Library, "Library Policies and Guidelines," www.jocolibrary.org/index.asp?DisplayPageID=1435; Sandra Nelson and June Garcia, *Creating Policies for Results* (Chicago: ALA Editions, 2003); Mary Y. Moore, *The Successful Library Trustee Handbook* (Chicago: ALA Editions, 2005).

20. Tippecanoe County Public Library Strategic Plan 2005–2008 (Lafayette, IN: 2005) 4 at www.tcpl.lib.in.us/admin/index.htm, then under "Library Board Policies," click "Strategic Plan 2005–2008" for pdf version.

21. Baltimore County Public Library, *Help Manual: A Guide for Emergency Situations*, section 3, "Problem behavior" (Baltimore: 1995), 3.

22. Based on items including *Fundamentals of Collection Development and Management* (Chicago: ALA Editions, 2004); James Burgett, John Haar, and Linda L. Phillips, *Collaborative Collection Development* (Chicago: ALA Editions, 2004).

23. "Protesters Greet Supremacists in Virginia," *American Libraries* 33, no. 10 (November 2002): 28.

24. JoAnne Pinder, former director, Gwinnett County (Georgia) Public Library, interview by authors, January 19, 2006.

25. Based on items including Mary Breighner, William Payton, and Jeanne M. Drewes, general editor, *Risk and Insurance Management Manual for Libraries* (Chicago: ALA Editions, 2005); Steve Cramer, "Core Competencies: Insurance," BRASS Education Committee, December 19, 2005, www.ala.org/ala/rusa/rusaourassoc/rusasections/brass/brassprotools/corecompetencies/corecompetenciesinsurance.htm.

26. Based on items including George Eberhart, "Katrina's Terrible Toll," *American Libraries* 36, no. 9 (October 2005): 14–25; Mary Cosper Leboeuf, "Ill Winds: Hurricanes and Public Libraries along the Gulf Coast," *Public Libraries* 45, no. 3 (May/June, 2006): 58–63; "Gulf Coast Libraries Get $17.7 Million for Rebuilding," *American Libraries Online*, June 23, 2006, www.ala.org/ala/alonline/currentnews/newsarchive/2006abc/june2006ab/gulfcoast.htm; Keith Michael Fiels, "The State of America's Libraries: Executive Summary," American Library Association, April 3, 2006, www.ala.org/ala/pressreleases2006/march2006/statesummary.htm.

27. Sharman Smith, executive director, Mississippi Library Commission, e-mail to authors, July 14, 2006; Sharman Smith, "When Bad Things Happen to Nice Libraries: Building an Emergency and Disaster Preparedness Program," presentation at the annual ALA/LAMA conference, New Orleans, June 26, 2006.

28. Based on items including Miriam B. Kahn, *Disaster Response and Planning for Libraries* (Chicago: American Library Association, 2003), 38–41; Johanna Wellheiser and Jude Scott, *An Ounce of Prevention: Integrated Disaster Planning for Archives, Libraries, and Record Centers*, 2nd ed. (Lanham, MD: Scarecrow, 2002); Deborah Halstead, Richard Jasper, and Felicia Little, *Disaster Planning: A How-to-Do-It Manual with Planning Templates on CD-ROM* (New York: Neal-Schumann, 2005); Chris Rippel, *Disaster and Emergency Plan* (Great Bend: Central Kansas Library System, 2002), via crippel@ckls.org; Richard W. Boss, "Disaster Planning for Computers and Networks," *Public Library Association, Tech Notes*, June 2002, www.ala.org/ala/pla/plapubs/technotes/disasterplanning.htm.

29. Johnson County, Kansas, Local Emergency Operations Plan, July 2005, www.jocoem.org/documents/LEOP/LEOP_(2005).pdf.

30. Maryland statutes, "Good Samaritan" law § 5-603, Emergency Medical Care.

31. Lee Brawner, former director, Oklahoma City Public Library, interview by authors, January 22, 2006.

32. Brawner, interview.

Local Values, the First Amendment, and Challenges

Quick View

Local values are fighting words. In many communities, local values are closely tied to quality-of-life issues and raising healthy, well-educated, well-adjusted children in safe neighborhoods. For most folks, upholding those values means engaging in a war on pornography and doing everything possible to protect kids. In fact, the many faces of "local values" cover much more than sex and reproduction. And every meaning affects your public library.

As tax-supported institutions serving the entire community, public libraries must balance local values with legal protections and rights. The public's fuzzy knowledge of what's legal makes the job harder. Blaring media coverage of the latest *Harry Potter* challenge doesn't help.

The issue is *when*, not if, your library will face accusations about ignoring both local values and legal protections. Being prepared can save dollars, time, and stress. It may also preserve the director-board team's credibility.

This chapter covers these topics:

- The many faces of local values
- Investigating community values
- Library staff values
- Board values
- Handling challenges
- Chapter checkup: "Clean Books USA Is on Line 5"

As explained in the preface, part of this chapter's content is on the book's website. That's where you'll find downloadable forms, lists of websites, and other sources. It also contains answers to the chapter checkup quiz.

The Many Faces of Local Values

Water is necessary for life. So is tapping local values for a successful public library.

Local values, a lightning-rod phrase, gets instant attention. It connotes beliefs governing how people raise their children as well as how they assess and behave toward one another. It is a land of passions, not academic debate. The list of perceived threats to local values starts with sex. Pornography, protection of children, and homosexuality constantly affect libraries.

Definitions

To many, porn is like art: They know it when they see it. Synonyms include *filth*, *smut*, and *indecent*. Pornography is defined by Merriam-Webster Online (www.m-w.com/dictionary/pornography) as "1. the depiction of erotic behavior (as in pictures or writing) intended to cause sexual excitement; 2. material (as books or a photograph) that depicts erotic behavior and is intended to cause sexual excitement." What one person considers pornographic, such as the nude marble statue behind a Washington official giving a press conference, may be seen as artistic or boring by another.

Three Illegal Categories

What's illegal? Three categories of "dirty stuff"—child pornography, items found to be obscene, and materials harmful to minors.

Child Pornography

It has been defined as a visual depiction involving the use of an individual under eighteen engaging in sexually explicit conduct. Federal law provides for civil and criminal penalties for

Sidebar 2.1. The First Amendment

The Bill of Rights, put in force on December 15, 1791, addressed ten issues identified as the thirteen states' conventions debated the proposed Constitution. Amendment I states, "Congress shall make no law respecting an establishment of religion, or prohibiting the free exercise thereof; or abridging the freedom of speech, or of the press; or the right of the people peaceably to assemble, and to petition the Government for a redress of grievances."

the production, possession, distribution, and sale of child pornography. It is not protected by the First Amendment, shown verbatim in sidebar 2.1.

Legally Obscene

This material is also not protected by the First Amendment. The Miller test, used in a 1973 U.S. Supreme Court ruling, still holds. It creates a three-part test to determine if an item is legally obscene:

1. whether "the average person, applying contemporary community standards" would find that the work, taken as a whole, appeals to the prurient interest,
2. whether the work depicts or describes, in a patently offensive way, sexual conduct specifically defined by the applicable state law, and
3. whether the work, taken as a whole, lacks serious literary, artistic, political, or scientific value.[1]

Harmful to Minors

Historically, state statutes have addressed this category. For example, the Arizona state code states that "'Harmful to minors' means that quality of any description . . . of nudity, sexual activity, sexual conduct, sexual excitement, or sadomasochistic abuse" that meets criteria such as "appeals to the prurient interest, when taken as a whole" and "taken as a whole does not have serious literary, artistic, political, or scientific value for minors." Note the similarity to the Miller test for obscenity.[2]

However, a federal definition was part of the 2000 Children's Internet Protection Act (CIPA). Under CIPA, that which is harmful to minors is defined as a "picture, image, graphic image file or other visual depiction." It prohibits on-screen depiction of material that is harmful to minors, in addition to obscenity and child pornography. In practice, CIPA's "harmful to minors" definition applies only to those public libraries that complied with the act to get access federal Library Services Technology Act (LSTA) or e-rate funds.[3]

The many gray areas of these three illegal categories often result in months or even years of allegations, lawsuits, court rulings, and appeals. In the meantime, what sure looks like pornography to Cyndi Citizen is delivered 24/7 by TV, cable, movies, print media, the Internet, and other media. For example, what used to be family TV time (7:00 to 10:00 p.m.) boasts top-rated shows such as ABC's *Desperate Housewives*, featuring scanty clothes and suggestive love scenes along with broad comedy and farcical plots.

Who's watching besides Cyndi? The Federal Communications Commission (FCC, www.fcc.gov) for one. It is charged with balancing First Amendment free speech against "indecent programming containing patently offensive sexual or excretory references that do not rise to the level of obscenity." However, the FCC covers only broadcast radio and television despite the fact that over 85 percent of all U.S. homes subscribe to cable, satellite, or wireless-cable TV. MTV, Cartoon Network, and others outside of FCC jurisdiction target young viewers with an entertainment mix including sex and violence.[4]

Others watch, too. For example, the Kids First Coalition prompted national steps including the U.S. Justice Department's Obscenity Prosecution Task Force. It also helped start the FCC's crackdown on indecent radio and TV broadcasts. One measure of the national concern? Congress's 2006 ten-fold increase in fines for airing indecent material; each violation now costs $325,000.[5] However, that financial measure of concern pales when compared to outrage over the Internet.

Library Balancing Act

That outrage makes a director-board team's high-wire act very difficult. On the one hand, as an entity serving a diverse community, a public library exists to provide access to diverse points of view. Library employees take that access, termed *intellectual freedom*, very seriously. It includes access to meeting rooms, displays, books, and other materials as well as to the Internet. At the same time, libraries must track local values concerning the content of those displays, books, and Internet offerings.

Laws cut two ways concerning intellectual freedom. On the one hand, First Amendment and other legal protections bolster library commitment to intellectual freedom. But other laws, especially state statutes, protect minors and others.

Your main tools in this balancing act? Policies, staff training, and a clear message about steps taken to protect minors while upholding legal protections of free speech.

It is hoped that the vignettes of actual incidents that follow will prompt your director-board team to review your policies discussed in chapter 1. Discussion questions might include these:

1. Have you provided the right policies to enable your director and staff to develop procedures to handle certain incidents?
2. Has your staff been sufficiently trained to react to and report various incidents?
3. Are your media spokespersons able to explain what is within and outside of the library's control?

These actual incidents show the range of perceived threats to both local values and protected free speech.

Porn and the Internet

The Internet's ubiquity, privacy, and especially its lack of content control are frightening when it comes to minors. From desktop computers connected by landline, DSL, or cable; from laptops in a wi-fi location; and from many cell phones, kids and youths can access millions of websites. The pornographic ones may include these:

- Images (still or moving) and sounds of mix-and-match sexual activities of all types and ages—humans, animals, inanimate objects
- Appeals or ruses seeking viewer information and participation
- Pedophiles trolling for children
- Predators seeking underage participants
- Sadomasochistic events and tournaments
- Paraphernalia and products
- Clubs, chat rooms, and groups

Listservs cover every sexual topic conceivable, including safe places to meet. For example, a small Michigan public library was notified by a patron that the library's restrooms were on a list of over 15,000 locations where gay and bisexual guys meet for sex. It took several months for the library, police, and undercover agents to end that activity. The library initiated some changes including the following:

- Two posts to the Listserv (one from the library and one from the police) that the library was not a safe place to cruise, and that the library and local police would prosecute any one involved in inappropriate behavior
- Daily monitoring of the Listserv to see if discussion regarding the library continued
- Installation of cameras in the hallway outside the restrooms to monitor who was going in and out
- Posting signs near restroom entrances announcing that the hallway area was under security camera surveillance
- Staff monitoring of restrooms on a half-hour schedule whenever the library was open
- Uniformed and plainclothes police officers in the building on an irregular schedule
- Police cruisers (not in service) parked in the library's parking lot

Eventually the postings on the Listserv ceased and patrols were stopped. Fortunately no innocent people ever walked in on inappropriate behavior.[6]

Where minors gather, predators likely lurk. The hugely popular teen social websites include Xanga, LiveJournal, and Multiply. MySpace.com, another Internet social network, offers music, personal profiles, message boards, and blogs that have attracted over 85 million teen and young adult members. The site has been ranked fifteenth in terms of page hits out of the entire U.S. Internet.[7]

Many adults, especially parents, fear that unsuspecting minors will be drawn into sexual or sadomasochistic activities. Statistics show that 87 percent of American teens have Internet access.[8] Forty-five percent of those ages twelve through seventeen had a cell phones that they used to go online or e-mail.[9]

Adults aren't being old fogies in their concerns about sex, violence, and dangers to kids. A national study showed that about two-thirds of teens age twelve through seventeen did things online that they wouldn't want Mom or Dad to know about. Providing too much personal information was cited by 79 percent of the kids and 81 percent of the parents.[10]

Spotlight on Libraries

Widespread fears about the Internet have resulted in federal, state, and local laws requiring libraries to take protective steps, notably installing filters. In 2004, 99.6 percent of America's public libraries were connected to the Internet; nearly 40 percent of them used one or more methods to filter public Internet access.[11]

CIPA requires filtering all Internet-connected workstations if a library wants to receive e-rate or LSTA funds (for more on the law and filters, see chapter 1).

However, the Internet isn't the only library resource that incurs the public's ire. Books, meeting rooms, and public displays also attract opponents.

Library Protests

Folks upset with their public library have many ways to vent their concerns. They can call radio jock Vic Vocal, complain to staff, fill out book challenge forms, contact the director, meet with the mayor, or corner a trustee at a church social.

In Texas, about fifteen protesters from the American Veterans in Defense of Democracy mulched seventy titles behind branches of the Montgomery County Memorial Library System as being "filth and smut." All seventy books, never listed by the group, were said to be held by the library system and available to children.[12]

In Utah, a free alternative newspaper became available again after back-and-forth protests. A patron's initial complaint about its content and cover stories had resulted in its temporarily being removed from the Provo City Library's lobby. However, another patron protested that removal.

A review of policies resulted in shelving all newspapers on the library's second floor, none in the lobby.[13]

Protecting Children from Sexual Crimes and Images

While some young mothers may see danger in every bearded male, libraries know first-hand that children need protection. A screaming twenty-month-old girl was rescued by fast-moving Des Moines (Iowa) Public Library staff from a locked men's bathroom. A registered sex offender was arrested for kidnapping and sexual assault; the babysitter had been only feet away using a computer.[14]

An attempted rape of an eight-year-old Pennsylvania girl resulted in a thirty-five-to-seventy-year prison sentence for a homeless man. She was attacked at the Free Library of Philadelphia's Independence branch. He had been kicked out of the library repeatedly for viewing pornography and publicly masturbating at library computers.[15]

Following a girl's complaint of being photographed in the library by a man with a cell phone, Plymouth (Massachusetts) Public Library staff checked an online Sex Offender Registry Board, then notified police. A search of the man's home turned up child pornography, although no photos of the girl.[16]

Sometimes counties require library actions to protect kids. In Florida, the Marion County Commission passed 4–1 a policy requiring its library system to set up separate, restricted shelves for books inappropriate to children seventeen and under. It also dissolved the ten-person advisory board, which had resisted earlier director decisions to remove the novel *Eat Me*. The county commission, per its website, then delegated daily operational responsibility for the library to the county administration.[17]

Homosexuality

For years, books on teen and other homosexuality have been challenged. The American Library Association (ALA) notes that between 1990 and 2000, 515 out of 6,364 challenges, or 8 percent, dealt with homosexuality.

In the next five years, 2000 through 2004, 128 (or 4.8 percent) of the 2,614 challenges dealt with homosexuality. *Daddy's Roommate* and *Heather Has Two Mommies* are just two of the better-known titles.[18]

While a challenge of an individual book gets attention, challenging a display can get even more. The entire Hillsborough, Florida, county government was forbidden to give any official recognition to "gay pride" due to a library's gay and lesbian book exhibit. After receiving complaints, the county attorney's office advised the Tampa-Hillsborough County Public Library to remove the exhibit, which it did. Later, the county commission voted 5–1 to ban all county government from acknowledging gay pride. Defining gay pride and the ban's application (for example, does it extend to purchasing materials? to meeting room use?) depends on the situation and circumstances, the county attorney said.

Next, the Florida Library Association passed a motion not to hold any meetings in the county until the policy is rescinded. The ALA censured the county vote. Then a lawsuit was filed against Hillsborough County by a Tampa strip-club owner, asserting that the ban was unconstitutional due to violating the plaintiff's First Amendment rights to get information at local libraries. As of July 2006, the Florida Library Association's "no meetings in Hillsborough County" policy was still in effect because the Board of Commissioners had not rescinded its direction that no county agencies can participate in gay pride activities or events.[19]

More Perceived Threats to Local Values

Do perceived threats to local values cover more than sex and reproduction? Yes, especially violence and religion.

Violence

From prime-time TV body counts to cannibalism in video games, violence sells, even to minors. The National Institute on Media and the Family's 2005 annual secret child shopper program found that 44 percent were able to

buy M-rated games intended for seventeen-year-olds or older, up 10 percent from its 2004 study.[20]

The Pew Research Center's ongoing studies showed that about 60
percent of Americans are "very concerned" about the violence and sex
found on TV and in song lyrics, video games, and movies. Library collections aren't exempt. Out of 2,614 materials challenges for 2000–2004
shown in ALA's database, 378 (or 14.5 percent) were for violence.[21]

Religion

Not enough books on faiths. Too many on the wrong type. Exhibits that
promote or demean a given faith. These and other complaints about
library collections are reflected in the ALA's 2000–2004 database showing
that 141 (or 5.3 percent) were for religious viewpoint. Another 220 (or 8.4
percent) were for occult practices or Satanism.[22]

Religious exhibits get extra attention. Three paintings depicting the
life of Jesus were barred by the Meriden (Connecticut) Public Library director. She cited meeting-room policy barring exhibits that were inappropriate or offensive to any community segment. However, the board reversed
the ban, inviting the artist to reschedule the exhibit.[23]

Religion affects library meeting rooms, too. After the Faith Center
Church Evangelistic Ministries was denied permission to conduct prayer
services in a Contra Costa County, California, library, it sued the county. The
church won an injunction; the county appealed to the Ninth Circuit Court.
Then U.S. Justice Department lawyers filed arguments saying that the
library must give religious groups the same access to public buildings as it
gives secular organizations. In response, county attorneys said that a meeting in the library was fine as long as there was no religious service.[24]

Other lightning-rod perceived threats to local value issues range from
environmental issues to animal welfare. "Poverty, health care and home-
lessness are moral issues" read a bumper sticker in Johnson County, Kansas.

Each perceived threat to local values generates opinions, emotions,
and perhaps action. Most impact the library. As a tax-supported institution
serving a community with diverse opinions, the library will never please all
the people all the time, but it needs to know their opinions.

Investigating Community Values

For measuring local values, one size doesn't fit even each major group. Slicing into community segments reveals further differences with age, economic, racial, ethnic, and other demographics.

Marketers of Al's Auto Parts or Zylia's Nail Shoppe mine federal censuses, economic trend studies, and other sources. Dicing by age, gender, family income, education, race, and nationality uncovers information about lifestyles by zip code and precinct.

Population Segments

So who's out there in our communities?

The veteran or silent generation. Born 1945 or earlier. Totaling about 62 million, their characteristics include doing their duty, no debt, stability, and conformity.

Baby boomers. Born 1946–1964. Totaling about 77 million people, many see age fifty as the beginning of a new middle-age phase. In 2005, boomers' average annual pretax household income was estimated to be about $57,000. Characteristics include going for the gusto, conspicuous consumption, winning, and competition.

Generation X. Born 1965–1985. Totaling about 82 million, characteristics include being with friends, risk taking, enigmatic ("whatever").

Millennials, Generation Y, NextGen. Born in 1986 on, totaling about 60 million. Also known as the digital generation. Their characteristics include tolerance, independence, making the world a better place, and optimism.[25]

Another important subgroup? The 24 million teens age twelve through seventeen, highly desired by marketers as well as libraries. Called Generation @ or MySpace Generation after the popular website. This age group breaks records for multitasking. They simultaneously IM (instant message) with one or more people, use cell or video phones, surf the Net, update their blogs (weblogs), play video games, and maybe even study. Characteristics include online social life and buying power. The estimated teen consumer market is about $175 billion annually. Thirty-three percent of high schools seniors have a credit card.[26]

Slicing by Gender, Race, and Ethnicity

Gender

According to the 2000 census, the population of the United States on April 1, 2000, was 281.4 million. Women slightly outnumber men, 50.9 percent to 49.1 percent. The male-female ratio (the number who were male times 100 divided by the number who were female) increased from 95.1 in 1990 to 96.3 in 2000. The relative size of the male and female populations varies by geographic region. The Northeast had the lowest male-female ratio— 93.5. The Midwest and South had male-female ratios of 96.1 and 95.9, respectively. The West had the highest male-female ratio, at 99.6, approaching parity between the sexes. More specifics about the male-female ratio in various counties can be found in *Gender: Census 2000 Brief*, www.census.gov/prod/2001pubs/c2kbr01-9.pdf.

Racial and Ethnic Groups Cohorts

According to the 2000 census, 75.1 percent of the population is white, and 24.9 percent is racial and ethnic minorities. The question on race was asked of every individual living in the United States, and responses reflect self-identification. The question for Census 2000 differed from the 1990 census in several ways. Most significantly, respondents were given the option of selecting one or more race categories to indicate their racial identities.[27]

- *Black or African American.* The term *Black* is used in the text of *The Black Population: Census 2000 Brief* to refer to the Black or African American population. The number of people who reported Black or African American was 36.4 million, or 12.9 percent. This number includes 34.7 million (or 12.3 percent) who reported only Black in addition to 1.8 million people (or 0.6 percent) who reported Black as well as one or more other races. People who reported Black as well as one or more other races were more likely to be under eighteen than those reporting only Black. The Black population is still highly concentrated. Sixty-four percent of all counties (3,141 counties) in the United States were less than 6 percent Black. However, in ninety-six counties, Blacks made up 50 percent or more of the total county population. Ninety-five of those counties were located in the South. More specifics about the geographic distribution of the Black population can be found in *The Black Population: Census 2000 Brief* (www.census.gov/prod/2001pubs/c2kbr01-5.pdf).[28]

- *Asian.* According to *The Asian Population: Census 2000 Brief*, the term *Asian* refers to people having origins in any of the original peoples of the Far East, Southeast Asia, or the Indian subcontinent (for example, Cambodia, China, India, Japan, Korea, Malaysia, Pakistan, the Philippine Islands, Thailand, and Vietnam). The number who reported being Asian was 11.9 million, or 4.2 percent. This number includes 10.2 million (or 3.6 percent) who reported being only Asian and 1.7 million people (or 0.6 percent) who reported being Asian as well as one or more other races. The Asian population was concentrated in counties in the West, especially in Hawaii and California. Of the 3,141 counties in the United States, 122 counties had Asian populations greater than the national average of 4.2 percent. The overwhelming majority of counties (2,382) had lower concentrations of Asians (less than 1 percent). More specifics about the geographic distribution of the Asian population can be found in *The Asian Population: Census 2000 Brief* (www.census.gov/prod/2002pubs/c2kbr01-16 .pdf).[29]

- *Other races.* The remaining racial groups number 25.2 million (or 8.9 percent): American Indian and Alaska native (0.9 percent), Native Hawaiian and Other Pacific Islander (0.1 percent), some other race (5.5 percent), and two or more races (2.4 percent).

- *Hispanic or Latino heritage.* The Office of Management and Budget defines Hispanic or Latino as "a person of Cuban, Mexican, Puerto Rican, South or Central American, or other Spanish culture or origin, regardless of race." The federal government considers race and Hispanic origin to be two separate and distinct concepts. The questions on race and Hispanic origin were asked of every individual living in the United States. The number who reported being of Hispanic or Latino heritage was 35.3 million (or 12.5 percent). Of these respondents 48 percent (or nearly half), reported being only White, while approximately 42 percent reported only some other race. Less than 4 percent reported being Black alone, American Indian, and Alaska Native alone or Native Hawaiian and Other Pacific Islander alone. The proportion of Hispanics within a county exceeded the national level of 12.5 percent most often in the counties of the South and West, especially in counties along the border with Mexico. Hispanics were the majority of the population in 50 of the 3,141 counties. More specifics about the geographic distribution of the Hispanic population can be found in *The Hispanic Population: Census 2000 Brief* (www.census.gov/prod/2001pubs/c2kbr01-3.pdf).[30]

Websites contain useful information concerning your community's racial and ethnic groups. They include the U.S. census, your local planning department, or your own library website. Understanding these groups may help you begin to tap into the values held by the members of your community, as many of the values people hold stem from their cultural, religious, or ethnic heritages.

Tapping Local Values

Users certainly tell libraries what they think. From a complaint to staff or a congratulatory e-mail to the director, the library logs them in and follows up according to library procedures. However, most libraries also use proactive techniques to assess opinions. Opinions of various groups can sometimes imply their values.

Director-board team, how many of the methods shown in figure 2.1 do you use? Only a portion of the form is shown; see this book's website for the entire downloadable form.

Libraries use many tools to gather opinions. Use this checklist as the basis for a board meeting discussion on methods and results.

Four main techniques help libraries assess community needs, which may imply some of their local values—an environmental scan, surveys, focus groups, and a review of community-wide priorities. Directors, it's your job to have staff execute these techniques. Trustees, your job is to carefully review the reports that are generated. Their data

Libraries use many tools to gather opinions. Use this checklist as the basis for a board meeting discussion on methods and results.

Tool	Regularly used?		Next scheduled use?	
	Yes	No	In 12 months	Not sure
1. Civic input during strategic planning	___	___	___	___
2. Surveys of users	___	___	___	___
3. Surveys of nonusers	___	___	___	___

Figure 2.1.   Opinion Assessment List (Partial Only)

can be mined for aspects of local values useful in reviewing your library policies.

Environmental Scans

The purpose of a library's strategic plan is to define the difference it seeks to make in its community. One proven strategic planning technique? The environmental scan. It allows the planning team to look at needs, statistics, trends, and emerging issues concerning its community and region. Data and opinions gathered typically include economic, social, education, technology, and research capabilities.

For example, the Cleveland Public Library used a three-part scanning process. Outreach to the Cleveland community included an advisory panel and town hall meetings. Input from library-based experts included peer review of comparable national and Ohio libraries. In-depth research was conducted on topics such as safety and security. The results helped inform its 2002 strategic plan.[31]

Local sources typically include stakeholder groups and their leaders, the economic development corporation, chamber of commerce, and school districts. State departments for education and for human resources can be fruitful data sources. One landmark study, *The 2003 OCLC Environmental Scan: Pattern Recognition*, might serve as a national benchmark for your local findings.[32]

Yes, conducting an environmental scan takes extra time and dollars. But your ROI (return on investment) starts with higher stakeholder confidence in the plan's vision and outcomes. The more population segments represented, the closer your library's strategic plan comes to meeting their diverse needs.

The second ROI is providing the library with shields against budget cutters. As discussed in chapter 4, sooner or later, city or county officials may try to prevent the library from getting needed funds. When Assemblyman Allen wants to cut out dollars for Spanish-language DVDs, you can show how the Hispanic community participated in creating the strategic plan. Your ace? Those participants are his constituents.

A final ROI? Showing employees that the director-board team didn't hatch the strategic plan by itself over lunchtime lattes. The folks who joined focus groups and answered the survey are the same groups that staff serve daily—young parents, providers of services to the homebound, the educational community, genealogists, and more.

Do tell the media about your strategic planning process and its environmental scan. Taken together, they show the library's commitment to finding out what people think and to identifying community characteristics, trends, and issues. Once that plan's approved, use every venue possible to communicate your vision, outcomes, goals, and strategies.

Surveys

Many libraries use surveys to assess community needs and opinions. The two main considerations are budget and methodology. Survey options include the following:

- *Media*—paper, telephone, or website?
- *Length*—short or long?
- *Design*—home-grown or hired out?
- *Data analysis*—done by staff, a local research house, or online software such as Zoomerang?

While the library literature includes many studies and guides,[33] three topics deserve special comment: nonusers, return rate, and benchmarks.

Nonusers. Why bother with folks who don't use the library? Because they pay taxes, may vote, and surely talk to others. One proven way to reach nonusers is through a telephone survey. For example, the interviewer starts by asking, "Have you or anybody in your family used the XYZ library within the past [number specified by the library] months?" If so, thank the person and go to the next phone number. It may easily take 300 calls to complete 100 phone interviews with nonusers.

Return rate. Research shows that a 1–2 percent return rate for an unexpected, national mail survey, such as one concerning use of disposable diapers, is respectable. However, libraries expect a much higher return rate. In our personal experience, a 30–40 percent library survey return rate is not uncommon. People care about their libraries. When offered the opportunity to provide input, many do so—especially when they are infrequently polled.

Benchmarks. Comparisons with your own earlier surveys or one or two peer libraries add perspective. Repeating some questions from your earlier surveys tracks how opinions have changed over time. Peer library survey results can be especially helpful if you both serve the same general geographic area. Why? People come to expect from all nearby libraries the best that just one offers.

Focus Groups

Many libraries use focus groups to assess community needs. The short definition of a focus group is getting feedback on four or five targeted questions, such as services to homeschoolers, from eight to twelve persons who know something about the subject, such as representatives of your local homeschool coalition. The facilitator probes interesting comments, permitting in-depth discussion of unexpected opinions.[34] For successful focus groups, review these dos and don'ts.

Do:

- *Recruit participants several weeks in advance.* Methods range from a form entitled "Want to be in a focus group?" at the circulation desk to inviting groups to send a representative. Recruitment is arguably the most difficult step in organizing focus groups, since it often takes several e-mails and phone calls to nail down the list of attendees. Be sure to phone all participants the day before, reminding them of the place and time.
- *Use tight time management that assures a maximum of two hours from the time participants enter the room until they leave.*
- *Design focus groups in tandem with your user survey.* The Anchorage (Alaska) Municipal Libraries used focus groups during strategic planning. "We had four groups—seniors, a civic group called 'Bridgebuilders,' teens and the general public," stated director Art Weeks. To get candid comments, only the facilitator and the participants attended. "We got invaluable information from these first-ever focus groups, especially the teens," Weeks stated. They were designed in tandem with a random telephone survey. "Our Friends and Foundation provided $15,000 for the random telephone survey. 600 calls were completed, slightly higher than needed for our population of 261,000."[35]
- *Write all participant comments on an electronic board or on a flip chart.* That way, everyone can see what the others have said. Often a helper performs this task, leaving the facilitator free to lead the discussion.
- *Be sure to feed them!* After all, they're giving that most precious gift, time.

Don't:

- *Assume focus groups are only for the big guys.* The Morrisson-Reeves Library in Richmond, Indiana, serves about 40,000 people. As part of strategic planning, it conducted four focus groups. Two sessions were with professionals serving special populations such as children and caregivers for the homebound. The other two were with education professionals and with families. One strong sentiment from the families' focus group? Assure the safety and security of children when in the library.[36]

- *Ignore shy or hesitant participants.* For example, going around the table asking the first question of each participant in turn allows all to answer. Depending on the group's comfort level, then switch to open discussion of other questions. Keep highly verbal participants under control! Facilitator comments such as "Jim, thanks for those several comments. Now how do the rest of you see this?" help get all to participate.
- *Forget to thank them with a follow-up letter.*

Focus groups are one power tool for probing target audiences' opinions and needs. Supersize that power when you pair focus groups with a survey.

Community-Wide Priorities

Do utilize a final source that should contain your community's dreams and values: the priorities shown in the master plan.

Some community-wide master plans may cover only a specific topic, such as cultural opportunities or educational attainment. Others may take a holistic approach, addressing several major topics such as economic development, labor pool, quality of life, health, recreation, and public safety. Whatever the scope, these plans will inform your own strategic document. For example, *Vision 2020, A Plan for the Future of Greater Lafayette, Indiana*, was carefully reviewed when the Tippecanoe County Public Library did its own strategic planning.[37]

If there's no written master plan, contact community leaders to find community-wide priorities. Your initiative about civic priorities will get their attention, perhaps surprise them. It's another way to help position the library as a community-wide player, as discussed in chapter 5.

Wherever possible, link library priorities and goals with these documents and priorities. Why? To show that the library will be a partner with business, governmental, and civic groups in achieving formal, community-wide goals.

Library Staff Values

Director-board team, regularly investigating your community's local values is essential. But so is understanding your library staff's values. No matter their job title or pay grade, employees are the single essential ingredient in making your library the best it can be. Library staff fall into two main categories. Professionals have an academic degree, often the master's in library science. Support staff have other formal degrees or solely on-the-job training.

Two Major ALA Documents

Both support and professional employees perform their respective jobs based on job descriptions, procedures, and other local tools that govern daily operations. Those local tools are almost always rooted in two very important national documents: the ALA's *Code of Ethics* and *Library Bill of Rights*.[38]

The *ALA Code of Ethics* sets standards, not requirements, stating that

> the principles of this Code are expressed in broad statements to guide ethical decision making. These statements provide a framework; they cannot and do not dictate conduct to cover particular situations.

1. We provide the highest level of service to all library users through appropriate and usefully organized resources; equitable service policies; equitable access; and accurate, unbiased, and courteous responses to all requests.
2. We uphold the principles of intellectual freedom and resist all efforts to censor library resources.
3. We protect each library user's right to privacy and confidentiality with respect to information sought or received and resources consulted, borrowed, acquired or transmitted.

4. We recognize and respect intellectual property rights.

5. We treat coworkers and other colleagues with respect, fairness and good faith, and advocate conditions of employment that safeguard the rights and welfare of all employees of our institutions.

6. We do not advance private interests at the expense of library users, colleagues, or our employing institutions.

7. We distinguish between our personal convictions and professional duties and do not allow our personal beliefs to interfere with fair representation of the aims of our institutions or the provision of access to their information resources.

8. We strive for excellence in the profession by maintaining and enhancing our own knowledge and skills, by encouraging the professional development of co-workers, and by fostering the aspirations of potential members of the profession.[39]

Director-board team, whether or not your employees have been to library school or belong to the ALA, its *Code of Ethics* and *The Library Bill of Rights* (see sidebar 2.2) permeate the policies and procedures of nearly all public libraries due to three major factors.

 Sidebar 2.2.
The Library
Bill of Rights

Since the mid-1940s, the ALA has adopted philosophical statements concerning local libraries. Premier among them is the Library Bill of Rights, which states,

the American Library Association affirms that all libraries are forums for information and ideas, and that the following basic policies should guide their services.

1. Books and other library resources should be provided for the interest, information, and enlightenment of all people of the community the library serves. Materials should not be excluded because of the origin, background, or views of those contributing to their creation.
2. Libraries should provide materials and information presenting all points of view on current and historical issues. Materials should not be proscribed or removed because of partisan or doctrinal disapproval.
3. Libraries should challenge censorship in the fulfillment of their responsibility to provide information and enlightenment.
4. Libraries should cooperate with all persons and groups concerned with resisting abridgment of free expression and free access to ideas.
5. A person's right to use a library should not be denied or abridged because of origin, age, background, or views.
6. Libraries which make exhibit spaces and meeting rooms available to the public they serve should make such facilities available on an equitable basis, regardless of the beliefs or affiliations of individuals or groups requesting their use.

Adopted June 18, 1948. Amended February 2, 1961, and January 23, 1980; inclusion of "age" reaffirmed January 23, 1996, by the ALA Council.[40]

First, they and other ALA documents have been adopted by reference by many public libraries' policies. Sixteen states have library standards that specify adopting ALA's Freedom to Read statement or otherwise supporting intellectual freedom.[41] Some board attorneys recommend such references, saying they help embed local practice in the framework of national and professional expectations and legal findings.

Second, many public libraries have a state or local requirement that at least the director has a master's degree from one of the fifty-plus ALA-accredited library schools. Not surprisingly, the *Library Bill of Rights* and *Code of Ethics* underlie much of that academic training. Those schools' programs range from degree programs (master's and doctorates) to certification (for example, the Public Library Certification program at Indiana University's School of Library and Information Science). Their graduates are steeped in library values, especially freedom of access to all points of view (intellectual freedom); reflecting community diversity in collections, services, programs, and staffing; and no discriminating on the basis of race, religion, ethnicity, sexual orientation, and so on.

Third, the tenets of the *Library Bill of Rights* and *Code of Ethics* are constantly reinforced through statewide and national associations, roundtables, and task forces. E-mails, websites, Listservs, and blogs help staffers from Seattle to Key West keep up. They cover local lawsuits, state and federal legislation, and much more. Daily desktop news about important issues and the ALA's actions is the norm, not the abnormal.

The ALA's Critics

The ALA's positions, activism, and lawsuits are highly visible in the library community through its online and hardcopy venues. The media covers it, too.

Proponents see the ALA's positions as the cornerstone of democracy in the United States and the chief provider of national standards for library personnel. But detractors see them as being soft on pornography, paying more attention to legal rights than to kids' safety, and being too liberal.

For example, in 2006 Oklahoma representative Sally Kern defended a bill that would prohibit state and local funds to public libraries unless libraries have "placed all children and young adult materials that contain homosexual or sexually explicit subject matter in a special area [and limited] distribution . . . to adults only." As quoted in the Oklahoma City *Daily Oklahoman,* she said, "And I will tell you this: The American Library Association is out to sexualize our children."[42] The bill passed the house, 60–33, but expired when the state senate didn't consider it before a deadline.

The ALA's positions also draw criticism from the library profession. "Do not assume that all persons working in the library profession support the sometimes 'liberal' views and platforms of ALA," said Susan Hill, director, Paulding County (Ohio) Carnegie Library in a program at the 2006 Public Library Conference. "And do not assume that if a librarian professes to be a Christian, that they are unable to provide excellent library service with a strong stance for intellectual freedom."[43]

ALA's *Bill of Rights, Code of Ethics*, and other core documents are reflected nationwide in local library policies and procedures. Many employees support them, but not all. For a list of the ALA's allies and antagonists and how to reach them, see this guide's companion website (www .pfisherassociates.com/scarecrowpress/sources.html).

Board Values

Trustees, what about the board itself? Whether elected or appointed, with advisory, partial, or full governing powers, what are your values?

Yes, discussing values is a sensitive area. Feelings could get hurt. Tempers could rise.

So why risk discussing them? Because values are the spoken or unspoken foundation for the nation's 9,214 public library boards. Knowing your fellow trustees' values will help you better understand their perspective and votes. The three main venues for discussing board values are strategic planning, board self-evaluation, and new trustee orientation.

Strategic plans must include a values section listing the agreed-upon norms for behavior toward one another. Those norms are unchanging. They apply to library users, staff, management, and the board-director team.

Creating that values section takes time and thought. Jump-start discussion by looking at other libraries' values. For example, the six values in the Columbus (Ohio) Metropolitan Library's strategic plan are these:

- Respect: "We respect our diverse, multicultural community of customers and coworkers, valuing the unique contributions of each individual."
- Excellence: "We strive for internal and external excellence in both our individual and collective actions."
- Access: "We are open and available to all."
- Flexibility: "We are responsive to the present and anticipate future needs of our community."
- Service: "We focus on our customers and coworkers and are committed to working on their behalf."
- Trust: "We expect competence, integrity and honesty in our personal and professional actions in order to earn the trust and confidence of our community and coworkers."[44]

However, strategic planning usually occurs only every few years. The board's own self-assessment provides another opportunity to discuss values, but this is an infrequent or nonexistent task for most library boards (for more on board self-assessment, see chapter 3).

New trustee orientation is the final likely occasion for discussing board values. That orientation, discussed in detail in chapter 3, provides the perfect opportunity to set expectations of new trustees by discussing the library's values shown in its strategic plan. Of course, other topics are also covered, such as the library's own policies and bylaws.

In summary, assessing local values makes Sudoku seem simple. It encompasses your diverse community with its many groups and subgroups. It also covers the library staff and the board itself.

Handling Challenges

Focus groups and surveys occur regularly. Orientation for new trustees and employees covers the library's values. So why do complaints keep happening? Books, the Internet, public displays and exhibits—the list of what upsets folks seems endless. Moreover, some people go past talk to putting that complaint in writing. Now you have an official challenge to address.

Transparency Rules!

To avoid the slightest appearance of bias, make sure that your entire challenge process is transparent. Then your spokesperson can say with confidence that the challenge to the teen gay story *Geography Club* is treated the same as all others. Avoid any murky steps that suggest unfair, unilateral treatment of this specific challenge.

Figure 2.2 shows the overall process of dealing with formal, written challenges. Typical components of the challenge system include the following:[45]

- *Lodging a formal complaint.* Is it paper only, or can patrons do it from the website? What happens to the form if the person doesn't want to give a name or address?
- *Tracking complaints.* How does the library log the complaint? Is there a database that shows its progress through the challenge system?
- *Reviewing the item.* Who's responsible for examining it? How quickly?
- *Procedures.* Where does your selection policy fit in? What status information does the patron get?
- *Administrative ruling.* Within the administration, who makes a ruling? How soon after the challenge was filed? How is the ruling communicated to the patron?
- *Appeals.* If the complainant doesn't like the administrative ruling, how is she or he advised on next steps? Does the board get an alert that an appeal might come to it? Is there a time limit on the board coming to a decision? What kind of documentation goes to the board? Is the complainant invited to attend that board meeting, to make a statement? How is the final decision communicated to the patron?

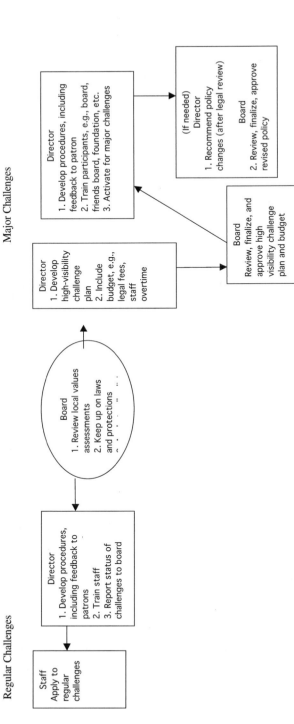

Regular Challenges

Major Challenges

Staff
Apply to
regular
challenges

Director
1. Develop procedures,
including feedback to
patrons
2. Train staff
3. Report status of
challenges to board

Board
1. Review local values
assessments
2. Keep up on laws
and protections

Director
1. Develop
high-visibility
challenge
plan
2. Include
budget, e.g.,
legal fees,
staff
overtime

Board
Review, finalize, and
approve high
visibility challenge
plan and budget

Director
1. Develop procedures, including
feedback to patron
2. Train participants, e.g., board,
friends board, foundation, etc.
3. Activate for major challenges

(If needed)
Director
1. Recommend policy
changes (after legal review)

Board
2. Review, finalize, approve
revised policy

Figure 2.2.   Managing Library Challenges

Will a transparent, carefully run challenge system result in a mollified patron every time? No. But it sure can increase the odds.

Dealing with Outrage and Outsiders

Upset library users who file a challenge are one thing. But sometimes, they don't act alone. They get help, whether before or after filing their complaint. Local and national groups can blindside the unprepared library system through e-mails, Listservs, and media campaigns. Out-of-state attorneys may join the fray.

In Kansas, the ALA *Bill of Rights*, *Freedom to Read*, and *Freedom to View* documents were for forty-nine years part of an appendix to the Johnson County Library's collection development policy. In 2004, one trustee objected to a *Bill of Rights* guideline that called on ALA member libraries to buy materials that reflected all points of view. Much media coverage and public outcry followed the 4–3 vote to drop that ALA guideline and two others.

After that vote tossing out the guidelines, the Plan2Succeed Citizen's Group in Chatham, New Jersey, sent a congratulatory e-mail to county and library officials plus the media. It said, "You have taken the correct action and I commend you for that. My group wants to make you an example for all the nation to see. . . . Please consider sending us something that other library board members can use to follow your approach and perhaps even get up the guts in the first place to stand up to the ALA as to the portions of its directions with which you disagree."[46]

At the next board meeting, when the objector was no longer a trustee, the new board voted 5–1 to reinstate all three documents. One trustee who changed to a "yes" vote the second time noted that strong staff support of reinstating the *Bill of Rights* helped account for his turnabout.

In another example, an out-of-state national group sought a local vote. Rev. Donald Wildmon's Mississippi-based American Family Association pushed for a vote in Holland, Michigan, that would have blocked the library's receiving websites that contained "obscene, sexually explicit or other material harmful to minors."[47] It went down by a vote of 4,379 to 3,626.

And in Kentucky, Brandi Chambless of the Broadmoor Baptist Church got permission to display a nativity scene in the community display window of the Bartlett branch of the Memphis-Shelby County Public Library. Later, a library administrator withdrew permission. The church then contacted the legal advice group, Alliance Defense Fund, which threatened to file a First Amendment lawsuit. Chambless also appeared on the national *O'Reilly Factor* in a TV program billed as "the war against Christmas." After urging by the mayor, the library reinstated the display.[48]

Remember, your crisis may be the number one topic in more than your community. It may be featured on the Listservs and websites of national groups. For websites of entities on both sides of library challenges, see additional sources on this guide's companion website (www.pfisher associates.com/scarecrowpress/sources.html).

Challenge Management Game Plan

If you thought bringing your first baby home tossed normal life on its ear, try a high-visibility library challenge. Everything happens at once—investigating the challenge, telling the library's story, and responding to inquiries. Expect nonstop e-mails, phone calls, messages, and media contacts, both at the office and at home.

How to cope? By crafting a challenge management game plan. Aspects to consider include getting advice, leadership, and legal review.

Advice from Library Groups

Start with two to three peer libraries that have handled high-profile challenges. What worked? What didn't? How did they use their Friends and foundation? How did they use their website?

Also, check out your state library association. Its website likely links to groups such as the Freedom to Read Foundation, People for the American Way, or the local American Civil Liberties Union (ACLU) chapter.

It may also contain helpful documents such as Kansas' *Intellectual Freedom Manual.*[49] Your state library can help, too.

Do use the expertise and many tools provided by the ALA's Office of Intellectual Freedom (www.ala.org/oif). Its decades of experience with the First Amendment, intellectual freedom issues, banned books, and court cases will enrich your game plan.

Leadership

A tiny group must be authorized to manage your challenge management game plan. In addition to the director, consider your board president, board officers, and public relations manager. Do specify who activates the plan—the director, board chair, or someone else? What happens if he or she is on vacation or out of touch?

The Friends, your foundation board, staff, and volunteers may all be asked to play a role. Make sure they get clear instructions about tasks, common messages, and due dates. Keep a regular flow of information going to all stakeholders. For a related discussion about leadership of advocacy to either protect budgets or get more public dollars, see chapter 4.

Alert to the leadership group: You'll be spending lots of time in your boardroom and not much on the golf course.

Legal Counsel

Have your attorney review the draft challenge management game plan. His or her involvement at the earliest moment is paramount since the challenge may go into round two, three, or even more, provided the will and funds to continue exist. Of special concern are steps to take—or not take—if the library is sued. The more your attorney understands about this challenge and your game plan, the better.

In summary, your challenge management game plan helps your library prioritize steps, request action from allies, and inform stakeholders. These plans don't cost, they pay off!

The Final Word

What must director-board teams have in common with ballerinas? The ability to balance in difficult situations while looking cool. Your job requires considering five often conflicting positions:

- *Local values*—community segments, library staff, the board itself
- *Local reality factors*—social change, economic development, upcoming elections, and so on
- *Community priorities*—as shown in strategic plans covering the city, county, or metropolitan area
- *Laws affecting your library*—local, state, and federal
- *Protections afforded to individuals*—local, state, and federal, especially the First Amendment

Whether a challenge is about a religious art exhibit or *The Chocolate War*, your director-board team must make a decision. Will everyone be happy? Of course not. Some will assert that you've ignored local values. Others will allege that you've trampled on legal rights and protections. Still others will go to the national groups or the media.

Is that the last you'll hear of this controversy? Only time will tell. However, having gone through a careful process of balancing local values with laws and legal protection, your team can take pride in having done the best job possible. That lets you turn to other strategic tasks such as those in chapter 3.

CHAPTER CHECKUP:
"CLEAN BOOKS USA IS ON LINE 5"

Your library's *Challenge Management Game Plan* named you as spokesperson. You just found out that Staci Stickler, whose husband is running for city council, was on Vic Vocal's radio shock show last night. "I filed formal complaints on six dirty books in the children's section," she told Vic and his avid audience. "They need to be removed immediately. Clean Books USA is behind us, too!"

1. Put these steps in the correct sequence (for answers, see this book's website).
   Sequence
   ____   Talk to Clean Books USA on line 5.
   ____   Get hold of the six books and Staci's written challenges.
   ____   Confirm that the *High-Profile Challenge Plan* has been activated.

More . . .

2. List two risks that your board must understand about this challenge:
   1.) _____

More . . .

3. Outline three short messages to use with the media:
   1.) _____

More . . .

4. Which of these rights are covered by the First Amendment?

	Yes	No
1.) Freedom of religion	____	____
2.) Freedom to bear arms	____	____

More . . .

Figure 2.3.   Chapter Checkup on Library Challenges

Download the form "Chapter Checkup on Library Challenges," which is illustrated in figure 2.3, to get going (www.pfisherassociates.com/scare crowpress). The website also has the answers to this quiz.

Notes

1. "Three Prong Obscenity Test," an element in the Supreme Court Decision regarding the 1996 Communications Decency Act, http://courses.cs.vt.edu/~cs3604/lib/Censorship/3-prong-test.html.

2. Arizona State Code, Section 13-3501, www.azleg.state.az.us/ars/13/03501.htm.

3. Based on items including Mary Minow, "Children's Internet Protection Act (CIPA)," August 31, 2003, www.llrx.com/features/cipa.htm, 14; Dick Thornburgh and Herbert S. Lin, eds., *Youth, Pornography and the Internet* (Washington, DC: National Academy Press, 2002), sections 4.1.4, 4.1.6, 4.2.2, 14.1.3; Amy Lisewski Lavell, "In the Name of In(ternet)decency," *Public Libraries* 43, no. 6 (November/December 2004): 353–59.

4. Eric Adler and Steve Paul, "America Debates Decency: Cable," *Kansas City Star*, August 28, 2004, A1, A18, A19(N).

5. Based on items including "An all-out assault on sexual content," *Business Week* no. 3960 (November 21, 2005): 118; "Major Roll Call Votes This Week: Broadcast Indecency," *Kansas City Star*, June 10, 2006, A8(N).

6. Christine Hage, library director, e-mail to authors, March 2, 2006 (library name is withheld to protect its privacy).

7. Based on items including Jessi Hempel, "The MySpace Generation," *BusinessWeek* no. 3963 (December 12, 2005): 85–96; Jenee Osterheldt, "Expanding Space," *Kansas City Star*, June 13, 2006, E1–E2(N).

8. Hempel, "The MySpace Generation," 85–96.

9. The Pew Internet & American Life Project, "Parents and Teens 2004," www.pewinternet.org/pdfs/PIP_Teen_Questions.pdf.

10. Pew Internet & American Life Project, "Parents and Teens 2004."

11. John Carlo Bertot, Charles R. McClure, and Paul T. Jaeger, "Public Libraries Struggle to Meet Internet Demand," *American Libraries* 36, no. 7 (August 2005): 78–79.

12. "Texas Vets Mulch Books in Porn Protest," *American Libraries* 36, no. 10 (November 2005): 21.

13. "Protests Prompt Provo to Reshelve Free Weekly," *American Libraries* 36, no. 4 (April 2005): 15.

14. "Des Moines Library Staff Rescues Girl," *American Libraries* 36, no. 11, (November 2005): 26–27.

15. "Library Attacker Gets Prison," *American Libraries* 36, no. 4 (April 2005): 20–21.

16. "Staffer IDs Sex Offender," *American Libraries* 37, no. 2 (February 2006): 18.

17. Based on items including "County Official Defends New Restrictive Policy in Florida Library," *American Libraries Online*, July 8, 2005, www.ala.org/ala/alonline/currentnews/newsarchive/2005abc/july2005a/marion.htm; Marion County Florida Board of County Commissioners, www.marioncountyfl.org/Library/LI_Funding.htm.

18. "Challenged and Banned Books," Background Information: 1990–2000, American Library Association, 2006, www.ala.org/bbooks/challeng.html.

19. Based on items including "Gay Pride Exhibit Leads to Countywide Ban," *American Libraries* 36, no. 7 (August 2005): 14; "Gay Pride Ban Prompts Suit," *American Libraries* 36, no. 11 (December 2005): 21; Ruth O'Donnell, executive director, Florida Library Association, e-mail to authors, July 21, 2006.

20. "Tenth Annual MediaWise Video Game Report Card," National Institute on Media and the Family, www.mediafamily.org/research/report_10yr_overview.shtml.

21. Based on items including "New Concerns about Internet and Reality Shows," Pew Research Center for the People & the Press, April 2005, page 3, www.pewtrusts.org/pdf/PRC_Apr05_Entertainment.pdf; American Library Association, "OIF Censorship Database 2000–2004, Challenges by Type," www.ala.org/ala/oif/bannedbooksweek/bbwlinks/challengesbytype20002004.pdf.

22. American Library Association, "OIF Censorship Database 2000–2004."

23. "Connecticut Librarian Bars Jesus Art," *American Libraries* 35, no.1 (January 2004): 25.

24. "Meeting-Room Appeal," *American Libraries* 36, no.7 (August 2005): 27–28; "DoJ Supports Prayer Meets," *American Libraries* 37; no. 2 (February 2006): 18–19.

25. Based on items including Patricia H. Fisher and Marseille M. Pride, *Blueprint for Your Library Marketing Plan* (Chicago: American Library Association, 2006), 14–18; Renee Vaillancourt McGrath, "Talking 'bout My Generation," *Public Libraries* 44, no. 4 (July/August 2005): 188–91; Louise Lee, "Love Those Boomers," *Business Week*, no. 3956 (October 24, 2005): 94–102.

26. Based on items including "Generation M: Media in the Lives of 8–18 Year-Olds," Kaiser Family Foundation, www.kff.org/entmedia/entmedia030905pkg.cfm; Jessi Hempel, "The MySpace Generation," *Business Week*, no. 3963 (December 12, 2005): 85–96.

27. Based on statistics from U.S. Census Bureau, American Fact Finder, Fact Sheet for the United States, http://factfinder.census.gov/servlet/SAFFFacts?_submenuId=factsheet_0&_sse=on; Denise I. Smith and Renee E. Spraggins, "Gender: Census Brief 2000," September 2001, www.census.gov/prod/2001pubs/c2kbr01-9.pdf.

28. Jesse McKinnon, "The Black Population: Census 2000 Brief," August 2001, www.census.gov/prod/2001pubs/c2kbr01-5.pdf.

29. Jessica S. Barnes and Claudette E. Bennett, "The Asian Population: Census Brief 2000," February 2002, www.census.gov/prod/2002pubs/c2kbr01-16.pdf.

30. Betsy Guzmán, "The Hispanic Population: Census 2000 Brief," May 2001, www.census.gov/prod/2001pubs/c2kbr01-3.pdf.

31. Based on items including *Cleveland Public Library Strategic Plan: A Blueprint for the Future of "The People's University"* (Cleveland, OH: Cleveland Public Library, 2002), 2–3.

32. Brad Gauder, "OCLC Publishes Environmental Scan," OCLC Newsletter no. 263 (January/February/March 2004): 1.

33. Ronald R. Powell and Lynn Silipigni Connaway, *Basic Research Methods for Librarians*, 4th ed. (Westport: Connecticut Libraries Unlimited, 2004); "Survey

Design," The Survey System's Tutorial, June 2005, www.surveysystem.com/sdesign.htm; Susanna Eng and Susan Gardner, "Conducting Surveys on a Shoestring Budget, *American Libraries* 36, no. 2 (February 2005): 38–39.

34. Based on items including Joe Langford and Deana McDonagh, eds., *Focus Groups* (New York: Taylor & Francis, 2003); Richard A. Krueger and Mary Anne Casey, *Focus Groups: A Practical Guide for Applied Research*, 3rd ed. (Thousand Oaks, CA: Sage Publications, 2000).

35. Art Weeks, director, Anchorage (Alaska) Municipal Libraries, interview with authors, January 22, 2006.

36. *Morrisson-Reeves Library Mission Statement* (Richmond, IN: 2003), www.mrlinfo.org/aboutml.html#mission.

37. Based on items including *Vision 2020, A Plan for the Future of Greater Lafayette, Indiana*, Vision 2020 Intergovernmental Commission, August 2001; Tippecanoe County Public Library, *Strategic Plan 2005–2008*, www.tcpl.lib.in.us/admin/strategic_plan_2008.doc.

38. Based on items including *ALA Code of Ethics* and the *Library Bill of Rights*, www.ala.org/alaorg/oif/ethics.html.

39. *ALA Code of Ethics*, American Library Association, 2006, www.ala.org/alaorg/oif/ethics.html.

40. *Library Bill of Rights*, American Library Association, 2006, www.ala.org/work/freedom/lbr.html.

41. Christine Hamilton-Pennell, *Public Library Standards: A Review of Standards and Guidelines for the 50 States of the U.S.*, April 2003, www.cosla.org/research/Public_Library_Standards_July03.doc.

42. Based on items including "Oklahoma Bill Ties Library Funds to Gay-Free Kids' Collections," *American Libraries Online*, March 17, 2006, www.ala.org/ala/alonline/currentnews/newsarchive/2006abc/march2006ab/oklabill.htm; "Oklahoma Senate Won't Defund Inclusive Kids' Collections," *American Libraries Online*, April 14, 2006, www.ala.org/ala/alonline/currentnews/newsarchive/2006abc/april2006ab/oklawont.htm.

43. Susan Hill, "Right of Center and Still Balanced," quoted in *Rural Library Services Newsletter* (May/June 2006).

44. *Columbus, Ohio Metropolitan Library Strategic Plan 2003–2006*, www.cml.lib.oh.us/ebranch/about_cml/sta_strategic_plan.cfm.

45. Based on items including James LaRue, "Buddha at the Gate, Running: Why People Challenge Library Materials," *American Libraries* 35, no. 11 (December 2004):

42–43; *Intellectual Freedom Manual*, 7th ed. (Chicago: ALA Editions, 2005), www
.ala.org.oif.

46. Based on items including articles, letters, and editorials in the *Kansas City
Star* and *Johnson County Sun*, April 23–May 26, 2005; Plan2Succeed Citizen's Group,
e-mail to Johnson County, Kansas, elected and library officials, April 25, 2005, for-
warded to authors.

47. "Michigan Town Rejects Censorship Plan for Public Library," *Church & State*
53, no. 4 (April 2000): 18.

48. "Creche Exhibit Resurrected," *American Libraries* 37, no. 2 (February 2006): 12.

49. *Intellectual Freedom Manual* (Topeka: Kansas Library Association, 2005),
http://skyways.lib.ks.us/KLA/intellectual_freedom/other_sources.html.

CHAPTER 3

Leadership and Management That Achieve Your Library's Vision

Quick View

What makes an organization successful? Leaders and managers who work as a team to get results that meet or exceed stakeholder expectations. For decades, experts have written, lectured, and consulted about leadership and management of businesses and nonprofit organizations. However, very little has been written on the dual leadership and managerial roles of public library boards. While boards must lead their libraries, there are times when they also have managerial duties. This chapter covers these topics:

- Why leadership matters
- Leadership and library boards
- Delivering benefits to your community
- Legitimizing a customer-benefits culture
- Effective board operations
- Chapter checkup: "Chairing Your Board's Self-Assessment"

As explained in the preface, check this book's companion website (www.pfisherassociates.com/scarecrowpress/sources.html) for additional sources.

Why Leadership Matters

Leadership conjures many images, from Winston Churchill in World War II to New York City's mayor Rudy Giuliani on 9/11.

Their examples fit the *Random House Unabridged Dictionary's* definitions: "1. The position or function of a leader; 2. Ability to lead; 3. An act or instance of leading; guidance; direction." The *New Shorter Oxford English Dictionary* adds "(b) the action of leading or influencing; ability to lead or influence; (c) the leaders of a group collectively."

"Leadership and management are two distinctive and complementary systems of action necessary for success in the volatile business environment," said John P. Kotter (85). That volatility is fed by factors such as technological, marketplace, and workforce changes.

The more change there is, the greater the need for leadership. Constructive change "begins by *setting a direction*—developing a vision of the future (often the distant future) along with strategies for producing the changes needed to achieve the vision," said Kotter.[1] The leadership activities needed to achieve the vision include the following:

- *Aligning people*—communicating the new direction so coalitions understand the vision and are committed to its achievement
- *Motivating and inspiring*—keeping people moving in the right direction, despite major obstacles to change, by appealing to basic but often untapped human needs and emotions

In contrast to leadership, "management is about coping with complexity," Kotter noted. "Companies manage complexity by *planning* and *budgeting*."[2]

Managerial functions include the following:

- *Organizing and staffing*—steps include creating an organizational job structure, communicating plans and policies to staff, and delegating responsibility.
- *Controlling and problem solving*—steps include monitoring results and solving problems.[3]

As noted in the preface, this guide uses a team approach to library governance with the director and board working in partnership in the roles of coach, team captain, and team players. This chapter stresses two aspects of the director-board team approach.

One aspect is collaboration. Instead of harking back to the traditional library division of labor whereby "boards make policy, directors implement it," we stress the director-board team using all the brains around the board table, not just one or two.

The second aspect of the director-board team concept concerns trust and confidence. Leadership isn't the exclusive turf of trustees, nor is management left only to the director. For example, directors let the board know when it's time to revise the strategic plan—and why. Trustees bring back new concepts and tools from state or national library conventions for local consideration.

Some readers may worry that assuming collaboration, trust, and confidence encourages trustees to stray into territory of the dreaded M word: micromanagement. Instead we see the director-board team's partnership as a proven method for dealing with constant change.

Director-Board Teams

Notwithstanding the military, the era of command-and-control leadership is dying for most businesses and nonprofits. John Carver saw the nonprofit board and its chief executive making up a leadership team. "Each can reasonably expect the other to exhibit leadership. If the board's job is well designed, board leadership is discharged by doing that job. But the quality of the design is paramount. Vision, values, and strategic mentality must be integral to the position."[4]

Speaking of libraries, Mary Moore declared that "the best relationship between board members and the library director is as a team working together for the good of the library and the community it serves."[5] Taking actions for "the good of the library and its community" means working to achieve your strategic plan's vision statement.

A library's vision states the difference that it seeks to make in its community and in the lives of its stakeholders. By working to achieve its vision, the library carries out its part of the social contract between itself and those who provide funds—taxpayers, donors, partners, and elected and other officials. Only leadership can articulate the vision and align the resources needed. Good management ensures delivery of those benefits to stakeholders.

Leadership and Library Boards

Two major factors hinder serious discussion of library board leadership. One is the virtual lack of studies about, or training programs for, trustees and boards. The other is the wide variance in powers of library boards due to state law, local ordinance, or bylaws.

Only Librarians Need Apply

In the library world, leadership studies and programs have mostly targeted directors and high-ranking managers. For example, Olson discusses enhancing customer services through leadership of staff that encourages shared accountability and responsibility. After examining over twenty library studies and reports, Evans, Ward, and Ruggas emphasized the A.C.E. (acknowledge-create-empower) paradigm that managers could use to help their staff learn about leadership.[6]

Some programs target emergent leaders. At the state level, the Maryland Library Association sponsors the Leadership Institute; directors nominate participants for the five-day seminar, who pay about $500 per person to attend.[7] The annual TALL Texans program, sponsored by the Texas Library Association, provides leadership development for midcareer library employees and others. Its intensive, five-day institute costs $550, excluding transportation. Participants make a two-year commitment, including pursuing a personal action agenda after the institute is held.[8]

On a regional level, the Mountain Plains Library Association (MPLA), which serves twelve Western states, sponsors a five-day Leadership Institute for librarians who have their MLS or equivalent master's degree and have a record of experience (including nonlibrary) that demonstrates leadership potential; it costs $450 for MPLA members, $550 for nonmembers.[9]

Nationally, the Urban Library Council's (ULC) Executive Leadership Institute utilizes workshops, personal assessments, and professional executive coaching as well as peer support networks that continue after the ten-month program is over. Participants are assigned a library project to manage and a mentor. The cost is $5,000 for ULC members, $7,500 for nonmembers.[10] Note that all of these existing programs are for library administrators and directors.

However, the ULC is discussing steps to provide leadership development programs to its members' trustees. One possibility is adding trustee-specific content and formats that would appeal to boards, such as funding, forecasting, and board efficacy. Another is providing opportunities to discuss "big picture" governance issues at ULC events. A third is creating a trustee Listserv. Another possible ULC step is integrating trustee-specific content into existing programs, publications, and workshops.[11]

The other barrier to seriously discussing library board leadership? The huge differences in powers, liabilities, and authority accorded to the three types of boards.

Varying Powers

State law sets the main boundaries for the board-director team by defining the powers and authority of advisory, full-governing, and partial-governing boards. To find relevant state laws, regulations, and guidelines, start with your state library's website and publications. For example, Wisconsin provides a series of twenty-seven "Trustee Essential" short white papers on topics like ethics and conflict-of-interest laws applying to trustees. In Kentucky, state law affords local boards with wide powers, including determining the library's mission and purpose as well as managing resources effectively and increasing them as much as possible.[12]

The main difference between full and partial governing boards? The former does its own financial management, ranging from setting levies and budgets to making investments. In contrast, the partial governing board must get final approval of levies, budgets, and investments from a city, county, or other governmental entity.

Other powers exercised by most full and partial governing boards include the following:

- Acquiring and/or owning property
- Hiring/firing the director
- Strategic planning
- Policy setting and review
- Evaluating director, board, and library performance

For advisory boards, a city or county administrator usually handles most if not all of the above responsibilities. The advisory board likely provides informal input, but the final decision lies with the city or county.

Advocacy, the Shared Task

However, despite their differing authority, the three types of boards share one major responsibility—advocacy. For this guide, advocacy has two definitions. One addresses shorter-term library concerns; the second, its long-term role as a community leader.

The first definition is causing others to support your goal as their own. This type of advocacy tends to gravitate to intellectual freedom issues, discussed in chapter 2, and to financial issues, covered in chapter 4. Whether it's fighting the mayor's threat to personally choose new children's books or getting votes for a $22 million bond issue, full governing, partial governing, and advisory boards must approve and participate in an effective advocacy campaign.

Fortunately, help abounds for this type of library advocacy. For example, the American Library Association's (ALA) home page menu shows "Issues and Advocacy," which links to the Advocacy Resource Center. Choose "Tools and Publications" to obtain detailed information and tools such as "Action Kit," "Library Funding," and "Materials in Spanish." Advocacy institutes are offered at nearly all annual ALA conferences. The Association of Library Trustees and Advocates, which uses the ALA's advocacy resources, has a special "advocates" membership category.[13] At the state level, library associations, state libraries, and trustee groups often conduct conference sessions and workshops.

The second definition is positioning the library to become a player in the community's power structure. "Players" help the library become involved in initiatives that are important to the community's decision makers. Over time, the library gets a seat at the community's priority-setting and decision-making table. This type of advocacy is discussed in chapter 5.

Leadership by the director-board team means very different things for full governing, partial governing, and advisory boards. However, all must participate in advocacy. Doing so helps them perform their team's three main leadership and managerial jobs: delivering benefits to the community, legitimizing concepts that help staff and stakeholders, and conducting board business effectively.

Delivering Benefits to Your Community

The first major director-board team job with both management and leadership functions goes to the heart of the library's half of the social contract: making a difference in stakeholders' lives.

Why say "stakeholders," not just "customers"? Because the latter word connotes just those who come into the library or use it remotely, whereas stakeholders include many groups—taxpayers, employers, elected officials, and so on. For example, GoodBuy Groceries has employees and purchasers who use the library; Don Developer knows houses near the new library sell faster.

Carrying out the social contract by making a difference in your community is not for the faint of heart. Winning the Super Bowl or Kentucky Derby takes preparation, resources, and performance. It's no different for the library director-board team, which must tackle three phases, each with major actions:

- *Setting shared expectations*—internal and external
- *Assembling assets*—attracting a top-quality director and staff; providing tangible assets such as facilities, collections, and electronic resources
- *Performance*—first, delivering needed programs and services; second, measuring and reporting the value received from them

Phase One: Setting Shared Expectations

Director-board teams must set shared expectations with two crucial constituencies: Your community via your strategic plan and your director through the annual work plan.

Strategic Planning

Most public libraries regularly update their strategic plans. For some, it's in response to state requirements. For others, it's a good way to do business. Fortunately, the library world provides them with abundant advice and examples.

For example, the Public Library Association's popular planning process starts with preparing to plan. It then moves to the community's vision and needs before actually designing and building the plan, based on thirteen library service responses. When planning, do keep the end product in mind. "In order for it to succeed, [planning] needs to be interesting, compelling and value-creating," said Frank Hermes.[14]

Library strategic planning virtually always starts with authorization by the director-board team. It usually includes community input and even community membership on the planning team. For example, the Columbus (Ohio) Metropolitan Library uses two-tiered "community-based" planning. Community leaders, a couple of trustees, and two or three senior staff make up the steering committee, which is responsible for producing the strategic plan. One unique factor is an advisory group representing various special interests served by the library; its in-depth discussions feed into the steering committee. This two-phase community approach, according to executive director Pat Losinski, "has a complexity to it, and our whole reason for this complexity is to give as much voice to the multiple stakeholders [of the library] as possible."[15]

Director-board teams, get extra return on investment from your strategic planning through transparency at every stage. Show how seniors, homeschoolers, the disabled community, and other constituencies provided input. Some may have been part of the planning team; others may have reviewed draft documents. Use the media, the library website, its blog, and speaking opportunities to show community participation and to get buy-in to the plan's vision.

Once the plan's finished, the director-board team monitors progress regularly. For example, the Olathe (Kansas) Public Library puts monthly updates in the board packet. Director Emily Baker reports the goal area, objective, action step description, responsible manager, and status as started, ongoing, or completed.[16]

Tip: Keep Commissioner Connie posted on her constituents' contributions to the plan. Their participation reinforces the fact that this is their library. The final plan bears their fingerprints, from the new children's room furniture to a coffee bar.

Director's Annual Work Plan

Internal expectations of the board and director should revolve around the annual work plan. "Why bother?" asked Trustee Tim. "Won't the director's job description be OK? We went to a lot of trouble to get it right!" Maybe so, but that job description is general, covering all aspects of the director's position. His or her annual work plan lists expected achievements. Mutually agreed to by the director and board, it forms the basis for the next director's annual evaluation.

Start by recognizing that the director oversees, rather than personally carries out, most tasks. One approach is a specific list of annual items such as the following:

- Get voter approval for the $22 million bond issue for a new children's library.
- Measure five outcomes from the current strategic plan.

Alternatively, the work plan defines major areas of responsibility, such as these:

- *Provide leadership toward excellence in service, management, and planning*—expand outsourcing from all fiction to selected nonfiction; increase program offerings in community locations by 10 percent.
- *Provide leadership in facilities planning, property issues, and construction administration*—acquire property for a new branch library.[17]

Ideally, the director's annual work plan results from collaboration among the director, board chair, and entire board. Sometimes, it reflects bottom-up input from managers, too.

In summary, an up-to-date strategic plan created with the community's help and an annual director work plan help set expectations that the director-board team monitors.

Phase Two: Assemble Your Assets

The second major component of delivering benefits to the community? Getting needed resources. On purpose, this guide discusses in detail only dollars, which in turn pay for staff, facilities, collections, and electronic resources (chapter 4) and personnel (this chapter).

Your library's number one resource? Staff! It's not databases, collections, or comfortable chairs. Getting the results your community needs starts with employees, from part-time pages to the director. Without employees, nothing happens. For information about other resources, such as collections and buildings, see your director.

Recruiting the Director

The library board has only one employee, the director. All other employees report to that person. They are recruited, hired, nurtured, evaluated, and sometimes fired by the director.

How to get Mr. or Ms. Right as your director? Options vary from hiring a national library executive search firm to do-it-yourself postings on your state's library websites or Listservs.

The tsunami of retirements threatening public libraries may chill your efforts. A 2004 ALA study showed the largest estimated retirement wave of librarians occurring between 2010 and 2020. Not only do directors retire, but the most promising internal candidate may be tempted by an early retirement program.[18]

What if the perfect candidate doesn't meet official requirements? If it's your own local library requirement, such as ten years' experience in a comparable position, you can likely waive it. State mandates such as having an MLS can be harder, but not impossible. For example, the Kansas City (Missouri) Public Library wanted to appoint its interim director, a former bank chairman and community leader who didn't have the MLS, as the permanent chief executive. At its request, the Missouri legislature changed the relevant statute. Other libraries having non-MLS directors include the Carnegie Library of Pittsburgh and the New York Public Library.[19]

Options. Most libraries seek a permanent director. But there's an alternative: the outside interim director. That individual gives the board some breathing room to decide long-term needs. Other advantages include having the outsider make unpopular changes quickly, such as staff firings or cutting back on duplicate print and electronic magazine subscriptions. If legal or fiduciary requirements were broken under the previous director's reign, the outside interim director works with appropriate officials to set up new procedures and firewalls.

However, critics warn that you may be hiring a person who interviews well but will cause new problems. Glowing references and glib comments may hide a management-challenged so-called executive who needs subordinates to get results.

Another option is outsourcing management, including the director position. Two firms in that business are Library Systems & Services, Inc. (LSSI) of Germantown, Maryland, and Information International Associates of Oak Ridge, Tennessee. However, contracting with them may be more than signing some papers.[20] A lawsuit by county commissioners challenged the Jackson-Madison County (Tennessee) Library board's powers to contract with LSSI. Its bid had indicated staff might be cut. A county judge said that indeed the library had the "authority to enter into contracts relative to the operation of the library."[21] Nationally, few libraries contract for director or managerial services.

Succession Planning for the Director

Any director, no matter how beloved or entrenched, may leave. More attractive offers, retirement, burnout—the list of reasons goes on. Hopefully the board and director have time to create a succession plan, permitting an orderly transition. That succession plan's two major features are the new director's expected achievements and the compensation package.

Expected achievements. Trustees, start your director succession plan with expected accomplishments, skill set, and character traits needed to get results. Do include time frames. As your wish list grows, make sure salary and benefits keep up.

Compensation package. What kept the current director on the job may not attract anybody else. Look at the directors' compensation packages of peer libraries. What's the salary range? Do benefits include a car, four weeks of vacation, and mostly paid insurances for the family? Those public library data are on most state library websites.

Do include funds for your director's professional growth through state and national association activities and committee assignments. Attending national workshops and conferences permits keeping up with hot topics as well as extending a peer network. For example, the Public Library Association offers in-depth preconference and regular sessions at its popular conferences and symposiums. And libraries belonging to the ULC can choose from several director training and networking events.

A director succession plan minimizes panic and problems when faced with a vacancy. But sometimes a crisis bursts, requiring emergency board actions.

Firing the High-Profile Director

Your board used a careful process to choose Dave Director. He gets a thoughtful annual written evaluation. The board and he together create his annual work plans. Compensation meets or exceeds peer library standards. He has ample funds for his community and professional activities.

Dave has become a community influential. His monthly "BookTalk" column in the local paper and "Read, White, and Blue" radio talk show are very popular. Now on the chamber of commerce board, he's started several useful partnerships with local businesses. And donors, especially rich widows, have enthusiastically supported his funding appeals.

But things are going wrong! Symptoms include the following:

- Escalating turnover at the middle-management level
- Inadequate packets and materials sent before board meetings
- Unfilled promises to provide better information to the board
- Staff leaks to the media about alleged morale and management problems
- Intermittent budget overruns

When the board's auditor told the board's chair of inappropriate credit card usage in six digits, it was time to act. An emergency call to the board's officers spelled out the three top priorities: protect assets, assess legal risks, and provide reassurance.

Protect the library's assets. Start by contacting the city, county, or library's attorney for advice on the following:

- Handling Dave's written contract, especially any firing and "golden parachute" provisions.
- Authorizing the library's second in command to take over.
- Deciding how and when to cut off Dave's access to financial and administrative record systems. Examples include changing passwords, PINs (personal identification numbers), and authorizing signatures. Physical facilities and contents need protection, too, requiring locks and combinations to be changed.
- Notifying Dave that he is relieved of his duties pending an investigation of alleged improprieties. Suspending Dave makes it easier to conduct the thorough investigation needed. It also gives all parties a breathing period for thoughtful decisions, not emotional reactions. Whether with or without pay will depend on your library's personnel policies and his contract.

Absolutely do follow your own personnel procedures, preventing Dave from alleging he was treated differently from other employees.

Legal risks. Minimize the likelihood of Dave filing sustainable grievances or lawsuits. Bring in an experienced personnel attorney at the earliest moment for this high-profile situation. He or she will advise on applicable federal laws as well as state statutes. Typical stages in a firing include the following:

- Written warning of failure to improve a previously noted problem. This letter of reprimand includes the possibility of removal from office.
- Negotiations between his and your lawyers concerning firing versus resigning, status of severance pay, and so on.
- Termination letter written by a legal or human relations expert that lists it all—the problem, the written notifications sent to the director concerning the problem, his or her inability to fix the problem in specified time frames, the termination date, settlement agreements, and so on.

Those steps set up a useful paper trail. If that trail is thin or nonexistent, Dave may have grounds for alleging an illegal termination. Make sure the termination is fair, consistent, and reasonable, complying with federal laws. That includes the Title VII of the Civil Rights Act of 1964, prohibiting discrimination on the basis of race, sex, religion, national origin, and so on; the 1967 Age Discrimination in Employment Act concerning employees over forty years of age; and the Americans with Disabilities Act, applicable to employers with over fourteen employees, prohibiting discrimination against qualified individuals with a range of disabilities.[22]

Some fired library directors file lawsuits. For example, in Michigan, the director filed a breach of contract lawsuit. His attorney said wrongs also included constitutional violations and defamation of character. The sole trustee who voted against the ouster resigned from the board, saying that the board violated the state's open meeting and freedom of information acts, and that board minutes contradicted the board chair's allegations.[23]

In North Carolina, a library director who fought his firing was rehired a month later. Over 1,000 residents had petitioned for his reinstatement. A mediator worked out the arrangement by which the director acknowl-edged there had been reasons for the firing. The Mooresville, North Carolina, town government paid for mediation costs and salary during the "unhired" period and awarded the director lost vacation and sick days for that period as well as $2,500 for his legal and insurance fees.[24]

Reassurances. Tell stakeholders it is business as usual while the inves-tigation proceeds. Use a board-approved message that the library is coop-erating fully with authorities to investigate the alleged problems. Create a sequence for communications with staff, community leaders, donors, busi-ness partners, foundation board, Friends' board, and the media. The sequence needs to include when Dave's e-mail access and voicemail mes-sage will be deleted. Alert: Make sure that staff do *not* hear this news first from the media!

Within the limits advised by legal counsel, keep up regular communi-cations with stakeholders. In addition to local media attention, do expect coverage by the national library publications such as *American Libraries* and *Library Journal.* Whatever some trustees may urge, do not hide behind "no comment." When you don't tell your story, the grapevine and Listservs will!

Boards and Employees

"Staffing?" asked Trustee Trudy. "Not our problem because the director handles it." Not quite. The director-board team undertakes both manage-ment and leadership tasks concerning employees. While your director is responsible for hiring, evaluating, and firing the other employees, it's up to the board to build the solid framework that attracts and keeps top rate employees.

That framework includes the following:

- Compensation packages of salary or wages and benefits compara-ble to local, peer libraries
- Personnel policies that set expectations about employee perfor-mance
- Support for continuing education and professional activities

- Periodic board review of manager turnover rates
- Good faith expectations of success with unions

Unions. Staff size affects unionization. One national online study of the staffing mix in 878 libraries found that 27 percent had unions. As the number of full-time employees (FTEs) increased, so did unionization. For example, 19 percent of the libraries with fewer than 50 FTEs were unionized versus 86 percent of those with between 500 and 749 FTEs. All responding libraries with over 750 FTEs had unions.

What about unions and salaries? Inadequate salaries and wages helped prompt formation of the ALA's sister organization, the Allied Professional Association. Covering both union and nonunion employees, it was established "to promote the mutual professional interests of librarians and other library workers." One purpose is the certification of individuals beyond the initial professional degree. The second is supporting comparable worth and pay equity initiatives.

During the Allied Professional Association's birth process, two library managers discussed whether unions could improve low pay issues. The Waterloo and Cedar Falls (Iowa) Public Libraries' director, Carol French Johnson, said the latter's staff is nonunion and is better paid; the city of Cedar Falls does a pay-scale study every ten years, so library salaries have kept up. San Francisco Public Library manager Cathy Bremer, who is also chief steward of the Librarians' Guild, Service Employees International Union, Local 790, stated that citywide salaries have increased 12 to 15 percent every three years since collective bargaining started.

From time to time, library employees do vote to join unions. Following a year of turmoil including staff layoffs, transfers, and reduced hours, professional and nonprofessional workers at the Providence (Rhode Island) Public Library formed a joint union on a 53–39 vote.[25]

Whether union or nonunion, MLS or not, the professional values of most library employees are grounded in national ethics and norms discussed in chapter 2. Through Listservs, local and state workshops, statewide committees, and national involvement, employees stay connected with peers in other libraries. Adopting "good faith" expectations shows that the library director-board team understands its union's importance in employee performance and work satisfaction.

Getting quality employees. Your director handles personnel management, but the board provides adequate funds. Those funds must include the cost of any director steps to attract, nurture, and keep high-quality employees.

What do library employees say keeps them on the job? One national online study gathered opinions about staffing needs from 1,890 public library employees. The survey listed three methods to attract a high-quality, diverse workforce (salary was not among them). In order, respondents selected the following items:

1. Paid student internships in public libraries selected by 1,424 respondents (or 75 percent)
2. Scholarships to attend accredited library schools (955, or 51 percent)
3. Job shadowing during daily activities (896, or 47 percent)

The best aspects of their jobs? Providing public service (624) and customer interaction (589). Interestingly, the least favorite parts were people (475), low wages (447), and bureaucracy (328).[26]

Tip: Review local area wages to see if yours are competitive. If WalMart pays more than you do, it might explain the high turnover in part-time circulation clerks.

Direct board-staff communication. The ironclad rule says trustees work only through the director. They never go directly to employees for fear of encouraging back-door communications by staff or micromanagement by the board.

But every rule has its exception. Sometimes the board needs to talk in person to staff about important changes and their rationale; it's not enough to hear it from the director. For example, the Arlington Heights (Illinois) Public Library suffered a cash flow problem that caused widespread changes. "Our director at that time informed us that our decision about cutbacks in purchases because of a cash crunch would be difficult for some staff to accept," said G. Victor Johnson, trustee. One of the trustees agreed to speak at an all-staff meeting, explaining the board's rationale. "That meeting calmed the waters," Johnson noted.[27]

Then there's the reverse situation, when the staff come to the board as part of an appeal process. If that appeal addresses a personnel matter, be sure to follow all steps outlined in the library's personnel manual.

Phase Three: Performance That Improves Lives

For decades, director-board teams assumed they were being accountable to stakeholders such as taxpayers, funders, and civic and community leaders if circulation and budgets kept growing. However, those statistics showed activity (outputs) but not necessarily benefits (outcomes). Then came a new federal definition of accountability.

Adopting Outcomes

In 1993, the Government Performance and Results Act targeted accountability by requiring every federal agency to establish specific performance goals, including objective, quantifiable measurements. At the same time, philanthropic entities were also adding accountability into their funding guidelines. The Institute of Museum and Library Services (IMLS) starting requiring libraries seeking its funds to measure outcomes. One library example concerning staff training shows the following:

> *Outputs*—forty-two staff members will complete training; participants will receive three continuing education units (CEUs).
> *Outcomes*—library staff will provide faster, more accurate, and more complete answers to reference questions.[28]

Next, IMLS funded the "Counting on Results" project, which designed and tested standardized measurement tools. Over 5,500 library patrons at forty-five public libraries in twenty states were asked about their actions in six library service response areas—basic literacy, business and career information, library as a place (commons), general information, informa-tion literacy, and local history and genealogy. The study found that age was the most statistically significant factor concerning use. For example, school-age patrons are most apt to use computers, whereas adults ages twenty-five to thirty-nine go to the library for a specific purpose or piece of information. Seniors go for a variety of reasons, ranging from attending a meeting to doing genealogy.[29]

Do outputs such as circulation statistics and meeting room usage still have meaning? Of course, since people do vote with their feet. Seeing trends in circulation and summer reading participation is useful.

But board-director teams that adopt outcomes-based evaluation take a giant step toward finding out how, and how much, library programs and services affect customers' lives.

At this point, you stand at the brink of creating "raving fans" by deliv-ering more than your customers expect through exceptional customer ser-vice.[30]

Delivering customer service is your director's turf. But the director-board team must review customers' opinions of those services. That means measuring outcomes as well as counting outputs through quantitative and qualitative methods.

Quantitative Measures

In America, numbers count. From kids' SAT scores to batting averages, folks use numbers to assess success. For libraries seeking to measure value received by customers and taxpayers, quantitative measurements include return on the tax dollar and customer usage.

Number one—return on the tax dollar. Show what taxpayers get in return for their dollar. The St. Louis Public Library used cost-benefit analy-sis (CBA), which quantifies in dollars the value to those served, compares benefits to costs of providing service, and summarizes in common termi-nology such as return on investment (ROI) and benefit-cost ratio. CBA's five steps are identifying and measuring benefits, identifying costs, comparing benefits and costs, drawing conclusions, and publicizing results. In St. Louis, households and families totaled 67 percent of the beneficiaries, educators and their students were 14 percent, and businesses and professionals were 19 percent. In 1999 the St. Louis Public Library showed over $2.50 in benefits for every dollar that citizens contributed in library taxes.

Two statewide studies showed impressive ROI for dollars invested in public libraries. In Florida, the return was $6.54 for every $1.00 invested; residents reported that they saved 57.6 million hours and $2.4 billion through using libraries. And South Carolina found that libraries returned $4.48 to the state's economy for every $1.00 invested in them; also, 47 percent of general users stated that libraries helped increase local property values.[31]

Number two—customer usage. Since people vote with their feet, statistics help measure value received. Just make sure you pair those statistics about hours logged on public stations with user ratings of those sessions.

Do add some pizzazz to the numbers. Did circulation of 600,000 children's and young adults' books set records? Tell folks that's the same as a Boeing 747 (at half a pound per book). Put a personal face on users' stories. When Hanna Homebound e-mails how much she appreciated mail-a-book, get her permission to share that story in the library's next annual report.

Qualitative Measures

Opinions reveal customer satisfaction with your facilities, services, and resources. Questions may range from reference staff know-how to ease of navigating your website. For details about surveys and focus groups, see chapter 2.

For a national frame of reference on customer opinions, check two landmark studies concerning user experiences. *The 2003 OCLC Environmental Scan: Pattern Recognition* found "a dissonance between the environment and content that libraries provide and the environment and content that information consumers want and use."[32]

To probe trends relating to libraries and information consumers, in 2005 Online Computer Library Center (OCLC) sponsored *Perceptions of Libraries and Information Resources*, an online, English-language international survey. It showed the low usage and image of libraries when it comes to finding needed information.[33] Sidebar 3.1 discusses the results.

Your environmental scan, focus group, or opinion survey, all discussed in chapter 2, may get results that differ from OCLC's. They may be very similar. Either way, its two studies provide benchmarks that frame your own results.

A different qualitative measure is professional recognition of your library and employees. Your library's excellence is reflected in local, state, and national awards and invitations for staff to be conference speakers. Being included in the annual "Hennen's American Public Library Ratings" is a noteworthy achievement. Put its logo on your library's home page.

Do get maximum media coverage for the library and for significant others. Feature Mayor Marsha praising librarian Randy Reference on his receiving that national lifetime achievement award. Provide similar accolades when Friends or foundation board members are asked to speak at state and national events. Stakeholders such as taxpayers, customers, donors, and others need to know that their library is recognized as a top-rate institution.

Value received is measured quantitatively and qualitatively. Whatever

Sidebar 3.1. OCLC's International Study of Information Consumers

OCLC's 2005 English-language international study, *Perceptions of Libraries and Information Resources*, got responses from 3,348 "information consumers" from Australia, Canada, India, Singapore, the United Kingdom, and the United States. Fifty-five percent or 1,854 were from the United States, of whom 75 percent had library cards. Findings include the following:

- Only 1 percent of respondents start an information search on a library website, while 84 percent start with search engines.
- What makes for a satisfactory information search? Quality and quantity of information— and search engines rated higher than librarians.
- The library brand is books, with no runner-up.
- Information consumers do use the library, mostly to borrow print books. However, they use it less since they started using the Internet.
- Search engines are trusted about the same as libraries.
- "Eighty-six percent of respondents feel confident they have the personal knowledge to evaluate information resources."[34]
- "Of the activities that respondents are doing less since they began using the Internet, watching television was number one (39 percent) and using the library was number two (33 percent). Reading books, the dominant brand domain of the library, was third at 26 percent."[35]

your methods, report the results fully. Help stakeholders see how your director-board team carries out its first major task: delivering benefits to your community.

Legitimizing a Customer-Benefits Culture

The second major leadership and management job of the director-board team is creating a vision or setting direction for the organization by defining the concepts and norms that govern daily operations. As a tax-supported service organization that seeks to make a difference in its community, public libraries need a customer-benefits culture. No, that's not the same as customer service, which targets the interaction of staff and users.

As used here, a customer-benefits culture paints on a much larger canvas. It assures legal protections concerning access to and use of information, while sounding out local values. It measures how well the library assesses and fulfills customer needs and opinions. Finally, the customer-benefits culture updates either its strategic plan or its implementation, based on customers' opinions.

How to activate a customer-benefits culture? By the director-board team adopting its three components: open-arms philosophy, change management, and values marketing.

Open-Arms Philosophy

The authors, one an African American and the other a Caucasian, believe that any customer-benefits culture must start with the rainbow of populations that libraries serve. But it doesn't stop there. The library's customers have differences and similarities of age, religion, cultural heritages, and political affiliations, just to name a few areas. In fact, even seemingly homogeneous populations have differences and similarities that could cause tensions. Chapter 2 discusses how the national library profession supports the library reflecting its community in every aspect—staffing, board composition, collections, policies, use of information, and facilities.

We believe that the library must also support the need to reflect the composition of its community. But we go farther; we don't think mere numerical representation in staffing and board composition is enough. Instead, the goal is to be open to and inclusive of the range of different points of view found in the community. We subscribe to the "salad bowl" metaphor of looking at the differences in our communities. Each element stands out versus blending in; and the result is a rich mosaic that can be savored.

We purposefully do not use the term *diversity* because we agree with Roosevelt Thomas and others that the term has become politicized. It has become a coded word that too often means merely achieving racial percentages in staffing that somewhat reflect community composition. Thomas masterfully articulated why he defines diversity as "the mix of differences, similarities and tensions that can exist among elements of a collective mixture" and a concept called "strategic diversity management (SDM)."[36]

For Thomas, SDM is a set of techniques for enhancing the way people make quality decisions in situations where there are critical differences, similarities and tensions. "A quality decision," he said, "is one that helps people and organizations accomplish three important goals: mission (what are we seeking to do?), vision (what would success look like ideally?), and strategy (how will we gain maximum competitive standing?)."[37] His work and our own experiences have influenced our views as it relates to libraries.

To be effective, the open-arms philosophy must be embraced and legitimized by the director-board team especially through its strategic planning process. The philosophy's components include the following:

- Reconfirming the library's commitment to legal protections concerning access to materials and facilities.
- Having regular contacts with as many community groups as possible—homeschooler families, storefront churches, youth groups and gangs, veterans, the disabled, service providers to special populations, and so on.
- Providing facilities that are welcoming to all community segments.
- Providing in-house or electronic access to legal collections and resources.

- Providing modern diversity training. The earlier versions raised consciousness about sensitivity; the new courses aim to give workers communications and management skills they can use in everyday situations.
- And, of course, staffing that reflects community composition.

Change Management

The second concept needed to achieve a customer-benefits culture is managing change proactively, rather than just reacting to it. Three important theories on change management have been applied to libraries.

The Learning Organization

Peter Senge's seminal *The Fifth Discipline* lists five factors or disciplines that are a catalyst for an organization changing itself. They are (1) systems thinking, finding patterns in the world about us; (2) personal mastery, creating the results you want; (3) mental models, beliefs and assumptions about how the world operates; (4) shared vision, commitment by the group to achieve; and (5) team learning, ongoing, simultaneous creativity between individuals and within the group.[38]

Looking at libraries, Joan Giesecke and Beth McNeil said, "Rigid rules, entrenched bureaucracies, and stable hierarchies will not help these organizations survive new technologies, tight budgets, competition and changing expectations of patrons and users. The concepts of the learning organization can provide leaders [administrators and trustees], managers and staff the tools they need to develop organizations that can succeed in turbulent times."[39]

Senge's *Dance of Change* addresses sustaining change in learning organizations. For a pilot profound change to be adopted by the entire organization, it must achieve legitimate authority ("governance"); "diffusion" throughout the organization needs supportive structures and practices; and a "strategy and purpose" must be adopted by all employees. The tools for disseminating that change are formal design, "the conscious, intentional architecture of organizations," and emergent design, the way people unconsciously "redesign their organization as they live in it."[40]

Appreciative Inquiry

Susan Annis Hammond targets organizational strengths and opportunities, not problems or threats. Based on the work of Dr. David Cooperrider and others at Case Western Reserve University, Hammond posits a "4-D" cycle consisting of discovery—begin by looking for what is working and "appreciating the best of our experience"; dream—consider what the future might be, "envisioning results"; design—what's the ideal?; "coconstructing"; and destiny—how to empower, learn, adjust or improvise, "sustaining."[41]

Looking at libraries, Maureen Sullivan found that most efforts by libraries to manage change used "deficit-based" approaches that focus on the negative.[42] Appreciative inquiry is a "collaborative and highly participative, system-wide approach to seeking, identifying and enhancing the 'life-giving forces' that are present when a system is performing optimally in human, economic and organizational terms."[43] For Sullivan, the principles of the learning organization track closely with appreciative inquiry. She concludes by saying that as library leaders contemplate "transforming their organizations, appreciative inquiry offers a means to do this that enables staff to affirm the best of the past and the present as choices are made to assure a future to which library services and programs are relevant."[44]

Communities of Practice

Etienne Wenger said that a community of practice (CoP) must have three elements: domain, community, and practice. Domain is a specific area of expertise that members share. Community is a set of people who interact with one another, who engage with one another, who talk with one another, who think together to develop relationships with one another in that process. Practice is ways of dealing with the problems typical of their domain that is developed over time.[45]

In a July 2001 interview with *Information Outlook* magazine, Wenger said that librarians can play an important role in helping CoPs organize the information they want to share. Librarians play and important role as a "broker," putting information seekers and information givers together. For example, the ULC has utilized communities of practice in its Partners for Successful Cities and Executive Leadership Institute programs, bringing people with similar interests and needs face-to-face as well as encouraging their keeping up communication afterward.[46]

How do these three theories help the director-board team? By setting a framework for its contemplating and handling change. They encourage diverse points of view, perhaps even heretical ones.

The outcome is brisk, perhaps even passionate debate. That's all to the good, as nonprofit organizational experts Richard Chait and John Carver saw it.

Concerning a nonprofit organization board's operations, Chait, Ryan, and Taylor posit two types of boards. The traditional board works briskly through a meeting agenda. A good meeting has brief discussion, mechanical votes, and little or no discussion; a good board doesn't get "sidetracked or fall behind schedule." In contrast, a generative board "promotes conditions that are conducive to robust discussion, enable broad participation and make discussion of generative issues everyone's work. The board moves from 'dis-sensus' to consensus" without having prematurely cut off thoughts or discussion.[47]

Carver also supported board members taking many points of view, noting that richly diverse opinions and discussion strengthen the final, official position that must emerge. As a "place of churning debate," the board is "an exciting place."[48]

Values Marketing

The third and final element of the customer-benefits culture discussed here is values marketing. The American Marketing Association states, "Marketing is an organizational function and a set of processes for creating, communicating and delivering value to customers and for managing customer relationships in ways that benefit the organization and its stakeholders."[49] In this guide, it is termed *values marketing*.

A key component of communicating value to customers is an organization's promotional activities. While libraries have talked about and carried out promotional activities for years, only recently has discussion turned to what is promoted: the library brand. A "brand" is a name, term, design, symbol, or any other feature that identifies one seller's good or service as distinct from those of other sellers. Organizations frequently establish the brand image by asking people what they free-associate with a given entity. What they associate with the entity is often promoted as the brand.

Strong brands are familiar, trusted, high quality, and relevant to needs. They are ubiquitous, clear, and consistent over time (even if the board and CEO get tired of them). Think Charmin and squeezability. When the brand works, customers remember it, repeatedly use it, share positive word of mouth, and refer others to the brand.

The OCLC study discussed earlier, *Perceptions of Libraries and Information Resources*, found that "books" are the sole library brand. That study also showed that reading books is a dwindling activity of the information consumers in six countries, including the United States. These findings suggest that libraries may want to rejuvenate the library brand by building a new brand image of "place," in which the library would be seen as a location or place to learn, support literacy, and provide research support, among other purposes.[50]

Directors have many marketing tools available to them. One business-based library marketing plan model uses elements such as the following:

- Target-market description covering items such as assumptions about target-market demographics and how members of this market use the library
- Current market situation, ranging from describing the competition to the nonmonetary or monetary price a customer will pay
- Marketing goals and objectives, based on the library's strategic goals
- Marketing tactics/action plan
- Implementation and controls[51]

Marketing advice abounds on Listservs, at conferences, and in articles. That advice includes creating a power mission statement that communicates the library's value, techniques such as catchy placards for use on public transit, and piggybacking on a statewide slogan such as "Missouri Libraries: Your Lifetime Connection."[52]

How does marketing pay off? By showcasing how the library uses funders' dollars. Marketing displays value to stakeholders, especially community leaders and influentials. It helps position the library as an important civic entity.

Marketing also reveals the library as a potential partner for non-profit and for-profit entities. Those partnerships can deliver new dollars or in-kind contributions, discussed in chapter 4. They also help position the library as a community player, not just a niche player, as covered in chapter 5.

In summary, the second leadership and managerial task of the board-director team is adopting a customer-benefits culture that embraces open-arms culture, change management, and values marketing. In other words, the team creates a "vision" and "sets a direction" that will inform and inspire daily operations and long-term plans for years to come.

Effective Board Operations

The third and final leadership and managerial job for the director-board team is effective board operations. Why mention the director at all? Because he or she is the front line for keeping you up-to-date on important local, state, and national library news and new tools. From ALA-family websites and publications to the latest OCLC studies, your director will select what applies to current or upcoming local issues. Some put "trustee education" on the monthly board meeting agenda.

For example, the Topeka-Shawnee County (Kansas) Public Library's ten-minute topics have included the budget process and the board's role in financial oversight. Per director Gina Millsap, the frequent staff presentations are held away from the board room, out in the library units. The board gets to see staff and workspace up close. Its all-online board packet, agenda, and supporting documents let Millsap e-mail hot links.[53]

This section addresses five major aspects of board operations: personal commitment; board composition, including term limits and succession planning; new trustee orientation; board productivity tools; and board conflict.

Personal Commitment

It's one thing to be elected or appointed to your library board. It's another to understand the commitment of time, energy, and personal reputation. The myth that "it takes only one hour a month" quickly shatters on the rocks of large board packets, emergency e-mails, and committee assignments.

Of course, variables affecting time needed include whether you'll get assigned to committees, whether the library faces crises or other time-consuming problems, and the average length of board meetings. However, our experience suggests a 1–3:1 ratio of preparation time to board meeting clock hours. Altogether, you're likely to spend four to six hours per month to get the job done right.

Consider carefully the needed commitments. Many trustees hold other leadership positions, to say nothing of details such as job and home. But time management is more than a balancing act. It also takes tools. Do you have a modern computer and telecommunications? If not, have the board authorize a loaner computer and pay for high-speed Internet access that includes plenty of e-mail storage on your server. You don't want to be handicapped in your intraboard communications.

Visibility comes with the job. Are you ready for criticism or even hostility from stakeholders? Can you handle starring in a political cartoon or a critical editorial? See the many examples in chapter 2 about controversies over local values.

Can you attend board meetings regularly? Some library bylaws define what level of absenteeism equates to resignation from the board. For example, the Atchison (Kansas) Library's bylaws state that "the absence of a member of the board from two (2) consecutive meetings shall be cause for the President to prepare and transmit to such member a letter of reprimand. Three such absences shall be construed as a resignation from the Board."[54] Seems harsh? Remember, your absence means your constituents or appointer is not represented in library board discussion or votes.

Board Composition

Heterogeneous membership aids vigorous board debate. However, the two existing national studies of library boards show them to be fairly homogeneous. One study was completed by the Association for Library Trustees and Advocates (ALTA) in 1997, sampling 1,200 library trustees in thirty-nine states. The other was done by the ULC in 2005; eighty-seven trustees from its member libraries in twenty-four states were interviewed by telephone.[55]

Both studies showed that the typical trustee was female, fifty years of age or older, college educated, and employed full- or part-time. Only one thing differed—the most frequent number of years served (mode), which grew from three years' service in the 1997 study to five years in the 2005 study. See sidebar 3.2 for details.

Sidebar 3.2.
Two National
Library Trustee Surveys

One study was conducted by the Association for Library Trustees and Advocates (ALTA), the other by the Urban Libraries Council (ULC). The ULC study addressed its membership, and the ALTA study addressed member and nonmember trustees. ALTA sampled 1,200 trustees; ULC did telephone interviews with 87 serving on members' boards.

Typical Trustee as Shown by Study

	1997 ALTA	2005 ULC
• Gender	Female	Female
• Age	50 or older	50 or older
• Education	College	College
• Employed	Part- or full-time	Part- or full-time
• Years served on board		
	Mode = 3, range = 1–35	Mode = 5, range = 1–45

Selected Board Information

• Method of selection	73.4% appointed	83.9% appointed
• Term limits	NA	2/3 said yes
• Number of members	NA	Mode = 7, range = 1–35

These two very similar trustee profiles raise the important question "What does it take for library boards to more closely resemble their communities in terms of gender, race, religion, language, age, sexual orientation, education, or other locally important attributes?" Two important topics are term limits and succession planning.

Term Limits

The intent of term limits is to get new blood and new ideas on the board. Who sets the requirement? It may be state statute, local ordinance, or local library bylaws.

For most elected boards, term limits mean not choosing to run again or losing at the polls. However, some states such as New York permit local libraries to set term limits on their elected boards.

For appointed boards, a typical term is three or four years, with one reappointment possible. Some rules permit a person to stay off the board for one or two years, then be appointed for a new cycle. In lower population areas, this proviso is important since only a limited number of people are willing or able to take leadership positions.

Ohio currently has no state-imposed trustee term limits on its 250 public library districts, but the concept has been warmly debated. The "pro" camp noted how trustees who've served for three or four decades often intimidate their peers and the director, taking provincial positions and resisting change. It proposed a state requirement for trustees to leave the board for at least a year after completing two full terms.

The "con" camp pointed out the difficulty in finding candidates in smaller communities. It felt that the current no-limit system resulted in dedicated trustees who represent their local communities. It also didn't like Columbus, the state capital, telling local libraries what to do. To date, the status quo prevails in Ohio.[56]

Succession Planning

Succession planning avoids scrambling to find a "warm body" new trustee. The key is listing needed attributes and skill sets ahead of time. Looking at the board as a whole, that list should include financial, managerial, political, and business experience.

Transition from business. Some business executives find the transition to nonprofit boards difficult.

- Don't confuse your personal enthusiasm for the cause with the ability to learn a new set of governance values. It's one thing to want to help single moms finish their high school education, another to put up with board meetings that discuss many, many other topics.
- Do realize that the nonprofit CEO practices little command and control and much facilitation and compromise. Help select,

nurture, and evaluate a CEO who deals effectively with a seemingly endless spider web of economic, political, and social interconnections.
- Do respect the huge importance of input by key constituencies. The power of many of your constituencies is rooted in social connections and public awareness, not money.
- Do help your fellow trustees size up an issue, discuss options, and come to a careful decision. As employers or owners, you make board decisions that have legal consequences.[57]

Recruiting board members. Practices vary concerning recruiting. At many libraries, the director handles most board succession steps. At others, the director-board team suggests names and also contacts candidates. Whoever does it, recruiting viable candidates should include the following:

- Setting clear expectations about the job; its time commitment; and tasks such as advocacy with city and county officials, strategic planning, and evaluating outcomes
- Describing legal and fiduciary requirements, including fiscal control and the First Amendment protections
- Covering current board facts about funding, advocating for the library with officials, and media attention
- Describing the formal process needed to become a library board member

The Kentucky Department for Libraries and Archives suggests that the recruiting interview include general library information, your own convictions about the library's importance, and current challenges and opportunities facing the board. Also ask what the candidate liked best and least about serving on other boards.[58]

Urge the candidate to sit in on a few library board meetings. It's one thing to talk about being on a library board. It's another to see it in action—from time management to the chair's handling questions.

Elected boards. State and local election regulations vary, but elections typically start with the filing of a petition or application form, followed by a public vote. But what comes before that? Finding viable candidates. The Maywood (Illinois) Public Library District board identifies users who have an interest in how the library works and the board's effectiveness and have demonstrated commitment to the community.

The board president then talks to those individuals, said trustee Rose E. Mosley, to see if they would like to become a library trustee and covers the process of getting signatures on a petition. If interested, they are encouraged to attend board meetings, visit the library, and ask questions. Then they get a packet from the library, providing information about being a volunteer trustee.[59]

Sometimes a vacancy must be filled between elections. The Indian Trails (Illinois) Public Library District keeps a list of people who have expressed interest in a possible vacancy. When a vacancy occurs, trustee Don Roalkvam reported that those persons are contacted, and then an interview with those still interested takes place.

The standard set of questions the Indian Trails interviewers asked of all candidates includes these:

1. Why do you want to be a library trustee?
2. Do you have the time to devote to monthly board meetings, monthly workshop meetings, committee meetings, library seminars and conferences?
3. Do you feel comfortable contacting local, state, and federal officials and legislators about library issues?

Once the interviews are over, the board meets in executive session to select the new trustee. The person selected to fill the vacancy must stand for election at the next local election.[60]

Appointed boards. For appointed boards, succession planning ranges from passive to extremely active. Some libraries just wait for Mayor Martha to send over the new name. Others encourage interested parties to fill out the city's application form. Still others recommend candidates to appointers.

At the Salt Lake City (Utah) Public Library, the director works in consultation with the mayor's staff concerning upcoming vacancies on the nine-member library board. Members are appointed by the city council for a three-year term and are eligible for one reappointment. Candidates typically have mentioned their interest to the director, noted trustee Roz McGee.

When a vacancy occurs, candidates are invited by the mayor to join a city council work session. Following an introduction by the library director, each elected official asks the candidate questions. Historically, only one candidate is presented for each vacancy. While Salt Lake has a rather homogeneous population, the library board's membership shows a diversity more representative of the United States as a whole.[61]

Of course, no matter how your library does board succession planning, you may not get your preferred trustee. Voters and appointers may select someone else. If so, welcome that individual to the board. Do everything possible to make him or her a valued member of your board-director team.

Tip: Do make sure the appointer is subsequently kept up-to-date on library matters. After all, that individual will likely be doing this again. To keep their appointers informed, the Wichita (Kansas) Public Library trustees use methods ranging from informal contacts to as-needed formal meetings. "It seems as though many library directors and boards fear communication with local elected officials," stated director Cynthia Berner Harris. "In my mind, establishing communications is the best tool for creating a great library. Once you tell the story of the library and the ways it serves the constituents, the opportunities for support seem to be much easier."[62]

In summary, succession planning is like buying insurance. It won't always get the desired results, but it sure beats waiting passively for lightning to strike.

New Trustee Orientation

Orientation's goal? To get the new person up to speed at the earliest possible time, able to participate in board discussions and decision making. Benefits of that fast start include these:

1. The newbie's constituencies have an informed spokesperson looking out for their interests and concerns.
2. The entire director-board team participates in discussion and asks questions, not just veteran members.

Issues concerning new trustee orientation include these:

- Who designs and does it? For many libraries, it's just the director, perhaps assisted at one or two points by the library's attorney. Others bring in staff to give specialized briefings.
- What's the content? Virtually all the state library trustee manuals emphasize the importance of new trustee orientation. For example, Wisconsin suggests starting with the board president welcoming the new person and scheduling the orientation sessions. Next, send the new person a packet including the state's trustee manual, board bylaws, a list of board members, and dates for upcoming meetings. The orientation itself should include a facilities tour. Meetings with the library director should cover topics such as library organization, governance, and funding; daily operations; and how the library could better serve the community.[63]

Michigan's library trustee manual urges an orientation that includes a building tour and reviewing documents such as the mission statement, strategic plan, policy manual, and budget. It suggests signing up for the State Library of Michigan's electronic newsletter. It also encourages joining the Michigan Library Association's Trustees and Advocates Division.[64]

Board Productivity Tools

With new members oriented, it's time for the director-board team to get to work. Three tools help to use time effectively: an annual calendar, board self-assessment, and board committees.

Annual Calendar

Directors, help your trustees look ahead. A year-at-a-glance calendar not only pins down dates, it also shows the flow of major topics. For example, November's strategic plan status review informs the February and March discussion of budget priorities. In April, the director presents a draft budget; in June, the final budget and its levy get official approval.

Other likely annual calendar items? Policy reviews, for example, the collection or meeting room use. Creating the director's annual work plan. Staff presentations, for example, website updates or services to homeschoolers. Naming the nominating committee and election of officers. The director's evaluation. Kentucky trustees are urged to scan their annual agenda, identifying lighter meetings where board training could be added.[65]

One bonus: The annual calendar lets all parties know of special, extra meetings such as a board retreat or a facilities planning session. The sooner dates get on calendars, the better.

Board Self-Assessment

Like many other organizations, library boards often are afflicted with group amnesia. They understand and verbalize the importance of accountability but somehow forget to do anything about it. In the midst of a busy year and new crises, there just isn't time to reflect on the processes and outcomes of their own work.

Why bother with self-assessment? To show that the board will spend precious time and dollars to look at itself carefully, finding out what isn't working and fixing it. Staff note role modeling. So do the Friends and foundation. It also sets expectations about desired outcomes of the next board self-assessment cycle.

Advice abounds concerning nonprofit board assessment. For example, Chait, Ryan, and Taylor propose measuring how well the board practices its concept of governance as leadership. Rather than asking if the board clearly delegates authority to the CEO or reviews the organization's mission annually, assessment includes asking each board member three questions. First comes "actual work" done in the past year such as attending committee meetings. Second is "valuable work," the board's tasks that are most important to the organization's success or mission, such as completing the capital campaign. Third is "meaningful work" that the individual would miss most, such as interacting with constituents.[66]

BoardSource offers a variety of workshops and online and print tools. Its *Measuring Board Effectiveness* builds on earlier work by Chait and provides results from over 250 nonprofit organizations that have used its methodology.[67]

Fortunately, library-specific board assessment models exist. For example, Dan Cain's method contains sixty-three assessment items in eight areas of operations such as board/executive relations, meetings, and making policy. Ken Haycock notes that monitoring and evaluating includes looking at the effect of the organization's culture and having S.M.A.R.T. (specific, measurable, accurate, relevant, and timely) objectives. Jeff Hixon's process evaluates four areas—the library, the director and staff, the board, and the individual trustee. It provides advice on the time needed to do the self-evaluation, which parts can be done in the board meeting versus alone, and tips on using the four worksheets.[68]

Some state trustee manuals also include self-evaluation tools. For example, Indiana provides a two-page form with yes-no questions concerning preparation for the job, meetings, individual trustee actions, and planning for the future. It also asks about areas of board strength and where improvements are needed. Georgia asks individual trustees sixteen yes-no-sometimes questions such as "Have you toured every library facility in the library system?" and "Do you accompany the director to budget hearings before governing officials and actively work to gain funding from a variety of sources?"[69]

What are some commonalities in these methods? Assessing the degree to which the board has the capability to envision and achieve a desired future. Checking its knowledge about state and local laws. Listing tasks actually completed such as evaluating the director in writing annually and making policies. Rating itself on conducting effective board meetings.

Evaluation shows your board's commitment to accountability and transparent operations. Unlike the U.S. Congress, which often exempts itself from requirements it places on others, your board will walk the talk by doing self-assessment regularly.

Board Committees

Practices vary hugely on the use of committees. Some boards work as a committee of the whole, except for occasional major tasks such as strategic planning or facilities assessment.

Other libraries have bylaws requiring several committees dealing with personnel, building, finance, policy, and long-range planning. They prefer recommendations brought to the full board by a subgroup that has carefully looked into options and issues.

Whatever your board committees, consider these aspects:

1. Are your state's open meeting laws carefully followed, regardless of whether the meeting is in person or a conference call?
2. Are alternatives identified and discussed carefully before you move to recommendations that will go to the full board?
3. Are notes and records kept carefully?

Whether your board operates as a committee-of-the-whole or in subsets, the key is trust and confidence. Trustees must believe that, regardless of the process used to prepare recommendations, the outcome will be a thoughtful decision. Using productivity tools helps your board achieve that high level of accountability you seek.

Board Conflict

Getting results makes all the difference with busy volunteer board members. They won't hang around long if they see their time being wasted or their integrity questioned. Board conflict prompts second thoughts about service and perhaps even leads to resigning from the board.

Roots of Conflict

Discussing conflict on nonprofit boards, Marion Peters Angelica identifies four contributing conditions:

- *Constant change*—this includes external requirements not under the board's control, such as new laws or funding shortfalls. Internally, it includes keeping up with technology and attracting qualified staff.

- *Diversity*—moving to a more heterogeneous membership can provide fertile ground for fallacious assumptions, misunderstandings, and conflict.
- *Limited resources*—stakeholders expect that the board, director, and employees will be effective despite inadequate funds, space, and other resources.
- *Innovation*—nonprofits are expected to find new ways to address society's problems despite those limited resources.[70]

Discussing a nonprofit's culture of integrity, Daniel L. Kurtz and Sarah E. Paul stress creating a code of ethics and conflict of interest policies. The board must especially keep up on the latest state and federal laws affecting conflict of interest.[71]

The Split Board

Conflict can morph into a more serious stage, the split board. Symptoms may include the following:

1. One or more members, often new, regularly oppose assumptions and decisions previously used. The rest of the board suspects a hidden agenda is at work.
2. Members regularly question the director's facts, analyses, and recommendations.
3. Issues are tabled for yet more study.
4. Tension and even rudeness dominate.
5. There is a typical reliance on strict parliamentary procedure, with which few trustees are normally familiar.
6. Open meetings laws are ignored, thereby excluding opponents on the board from discussion or voting.
7. Attendance is spotty, or members who are fed up resign from the board.
8. There is ongoing media coverage and increased attendance by the public.

Looking at school boards, Linda J. Dawson and Randy Quinn's checklist of destructive board member behaviors included "passive-aggressive

behavior, including refusal to participate during meetings but openly criticizing the board's decision afterwards" and "publicly criticizing the board
or the superintendent with the intent of promoting yourself and under-
mining public confidence in colleagues."[72]

Do these destructive behaviors occur in library land? Yes. In
Libertyville, Illinois, a vocal trustee was censured by the Cook Memorial
Public Library board for personally confiscating a free alternative newspaper issue. The trustee had also published a letter in the local paper criticizing the library director's permissive attitude and urging parents to beware
library materials. At the meeting where censure was voted 5–2, about 100
people attended; the 23 who spoke out were evenly split.

Five months later, the censured trustee and another member
opposed renewing the Cook Memorial board's ethics policy. They objected
to a portion requiring board members to abide by majority decisions even
if they disagreed, saying it limited their free speech. The board president
disagreed, stating that the ethics statement would hopefully result in civil
actions and respect of board decisions.[73]

Coping with the Split Board

Whatever steps the board chair, director, and other board members take to
address a split board, it won't be easy or fast. The points listed here only
touch the iceberg's top. All of them assume that the board chair and director talk regularly about ways to address the problem.

No matter what's done, the split may continue to grow until some
board members resign or are replaced when their term is up, or, where
legally possible, a recall election forces them off the board. Possible steps
include the following:

1. *Speak privately with the chief dissident.* Ask why he or she is upset
   and what specific changes he or she would like to see. At that session, the chair would also review the board's leadership responsibilities, policies, and processes.

   Follow up by speaking with the director; some of the grievances may reflect situations that need fixing. If the situation persists,
   suggest that the person resign. Jan Masoka noted that "sometimes
   problem board members are relieved to have this as an option."[74]

2. *Conduct a board retreat.* Hire an outside facilitator to help the entire board look at its culture and its work, identifying strengths, weaknesses, opportunities, and threats of both. Within Sunshine Law requirements, stress that the retreat is a safe zone in which participants will respect one another's privacy. Identifying both points of agreement and those of opposition helps all parties at least know where each stands.

3. *Use committees.* Assign the individual to one or more committees, thereby providing him or her an opportunity to work in depth at a library issue such as facilities planning. In this smaller group, people get to know each other better, permitting bonding opportunities not possible in the formal board meeting.

4. *Hold a legal review.* Bring in the board's attorney to give a refresher course to all parties on conflict of interest as well as state and local laws and requirements. Point out the liabilities for not meeting those requirements, especially those incurred by the board and, where applicable, those by individual trustees.

5. *Follow meeting procedures.* Provide a refresher course on Roberts Rules of Order. Replace casual decision making with a careful process for handling motions and amendments, getting seconds where needed, and calling for the question.

6. *Provide board training.* As part of board meetings, schedule brief ten- to fifteen-minute continuing education sessions on timely topics such as your state's public library standards and conflict of interest laws.

7. *Get comprehensive director recommendations.* Directors, minimize the opportunity for trustee nitpicking by presenting thorough recommendations. Include a statement of need, statistical and other research done, major options, and rationale.

8. *Ensure visibility.* Provide the media with backgrounder facts and a draft press release. Authorize a library spokesperson to work with the media, helping to counterbalance the dissident's opinions and allegations.

These steps aren't easy. Emotional pendulums are hard to stop. Perceived rudeness begets the same in others. However, it does no good and much harm for emotional responses to take over, especially when the media gives front-page coverage.

Get help from experts, such as a facilitator for that board retreat, an attorney, or a public relations advisor. Check out associations or university institutes that work with troubled nonprofit boards. Be sure to contact your regional or cooperative system and your state library. Handling the split board isn't for do-it-yourselfers. Get professional help.

The Final Word

The library board-director team has three main leadership and managerial tasks: delivering benefits to the community, legitimizing a customer-benefits culture, and assuring effective board operations.

Leadership and management are hard but rewarding work. Hearing homeschool families praise the children's collection or seniors laud and describe using genealogy databases from home makes it all worthwhile. When your library director-board team does the job right, your community reaps priceless benefits: the information and resources to pursue economic well-being, lifelong learning, and personal interests.

However, that information and those resources take money. Providing those community benefits means getting and growing the funding your library needs, covered in chapter 4.

CHAPTER CHECKUP:
"CHAIRING YOUR BOARD'S SELF-ASSESSMENT"

At last night's board meeting, you were named chair of the first-ever board self-assessment. New trustee Sarah Serious, head of the homeschool coalition, wants to make sure it's a board process and not dominated by Director Dorthea. Sarah has e-mailed you several websites on nonprofit and church board self-assessment. At last night's break, trustee Val Veteran whispered that it's all a waste of time.

At next month's board meeting, you are to present two to three possible self-assessment methods. Download this form, "Chapter Checkup for Board Self-Assessment," which is illustrated in figure 3.1, to get started (http://www.pfisherassociates.com/scarecrowpress). The website also has the answers to this quiz.

1. List the two board benefits you see from doing self-assessment.
   1.) _____

More . . .

2. Decide the sequence you'll use to find some library board self-assessment forms.
   ___   Look at your state's trustee manual.
   ___   Contact the board chair at two to three peer libraries to see if they've done any recently.
   ___   Contact the facilitator who helped your library in its last strategic planning cycle.

More . . .

3. You have thirty minutes to make your report and take questions. What will you cover?

	Yes	No
1.) Sample forms	___	___
2.) Experiences of other boards in doing a self-assessment	___	___
3.) Comparison of the two to three methods	___	___

More . . .

Figure 3.1.   Chapter Checkup Board Self-Assessment

Notes

1. John P. Kotter, "What Leaders Do," *Harvard Business Review* 79, no. 11 (December 2001): 86.

2. Kotter, "What Leaders Do," 86.

3. Kotter, "What Leaders Do," 85–97.

4. John Carver, *Boards That Make a Difference*, 3rd ed. (San Francisco: Jossey-Bass, 2006), 29–32, 176–78.

5. Mary Y. Moore, *The Successful Library Trustee Handbook* (Chicago: American Library Association, 2005), 72.

6. Based on items including Christi A. Olson, *Winning with Library Leadership* (Chicago: ALA Editions, 2004); G. Edward Evans, Patricia Layzell Ward, and Bendik Ruggas, *Management Basics for Information Professionals* (New York: Neal-Schumann, 2000), 361.

7. Maryland Library Leadership Institute, www.mdlib.org/leadership/mllihist.html.

8. TALL Texans Leadership Development Institute, www.txla.org/groups/talltex/tallldi.html.

9. Mountain Plains Library Association, www.mpla.us/, click "Leadership Institute" on the home page menu.

10. Urban Libraries Council Executive Leadership Institute, www.urban libraries.org/showcase/eli.html.

11. Martin Gomez, executive director, Urban Libraries Council, e-mail to authors, August 1, 2006.

12. Based on items including "Trustee Essentials: A Handbook for Wisconsin Public Library Trustees," http://dpi.wi.gov/pld/handbook.html; "Trustee Job Description: Major Responsibilities," *T3: Trustee Training Tips* 1, no. 7 (Spring 2006): 3.

13. Based on items including American Library Association, Advocacy Resource Center, www.ala.org/ala/issues/issuesadvocacy.htm; Ellen Miller, "Advocacy ABCs for Library Trustees," *American Libraries* 32, no. 8 (September, 2001): 56–59.

14. Frank Hermes, "Strategic Planning Part 2: Planning for Planning," *The Library Leadership Network*, August 16, 2006, www.libraryleadership.net, click "Strategic Planning Series," then scroll down and select the "Planning for Planning" article; based on items including Sandra Nelson, *The New Planning for Results* (Chicago: American Library Association, 2001), 65; Edward J. Elsner, "The Evolution of PLA's Planning Model," *Public Libraries* 41, no. 4 (July/August 2002): 209–15; Deborah Kocsis and Sue Waechter, *Driving Strategic Planning* (Hoboken, NJ: John Wiley & Sons, 2003).

15. Frank Hermes, "Managing #1," quoting Pat Losinski, executive director, Columbus (Ohio) Metropolitan Library, as published in *The Library Leadership Network*, June 22, 2006, www.libraryleadership.net, click "Archives," then click "May/June 2006"; scroll down and select "Managing Number One," which is labeled *free*.

16. Emily Baker, director, Olathe (Kansas) Public Library, interview with authors, June 9, 2006.

17. Mona Carmack, librarian, Johnson County (Kansas) e-mail to authors, April 12, 2006.

18. Based on items including "Library Retirements: What Can We Expect," *American Libraries* 36, no. 8 (September 2005): 16; Ellen G. Miller, "Retirement Tsunami Looms over Distracted Director/Board Teams," *Public Libraries* 43, no. 2 (March–April 2004): 77.

19. Detroit Suburban Librarians' Roundtable, *A Library Board's Practical Guide to Finding the Right Library Director* (Chicago: Public Library Association, 2005); James Hart, "Library's Search Takes a Broad View," *Kansas City Star*, December 14, 2004, B1(N).

20. Based on items including James B. Casey, "Beware the Itinerant Director," *American Libraries* 35, no. 6 (June/July 2004): 52–54; Leslie R. Morris, "The Case for an Outside Interim Director," *American Libraries* 35, no. 6 (June/July 2004): 52–54.

21. "Tennessee Judge Rules Library Can Privatize," *American Libraries Online*, August 11, 2006, www.ala.org/ala/alonline/currentnews/newsarchive/2006abc/august2006a/jackson.htm.

22. Based on items including Carol E. Weisman, *Losing Your Executive Director without Losing Your Way* (San Francisco: Jossey-Bass, 2004), 21–25, 41–45; Mary Y. Moore, *The Successful Library Trustee Handbook* (Chicago: American Library Association, 2005), 67–69.

23. "Fired Michigan Director Will File Lawsuit," *American Libraries Online*, April 7, 2006, www.ala.org/ala/alonline/currentnews/newsarchive/2006abc/april2006ab/baycounty.htm.

24. "Mooresville Director Back," *American Libraries* 35, no. 9 (October 2004): 19.

25. Jeanne Goodrich, "Staffing Public Libraries," *Public Libraries* 44, no. 5 (September/October, 2005): 277–81; "Can Unions Solve the Low-Pay Dilemma?" *American Libraries* 33, no. 1 (January 2002): 65–69; "Providence Public Library Staff Votes to Unionize," *American Libraries* 36, no. 9 (October, 2005): 26.

26. Based on "What Are They Thinking?" *Public Libraries* 45, no. 1 (January/February 2006): 53–57.

27. G. Victor Johnson, trustee, Arlington Heights (Illinois) Public Library, e-mail to authors, March 6, 2006.

28. Based on items including Peggy D. Rudd, "Documenting the Difference: Demonstrating the Value of Libraries through Outcome Measurements," in *Perspectives on Outcome Based Evaluation for Libraries and Museums*: 16, www.imls.gov/pdf/pubobe.pdf; Institute of Museum and Library Services, "Frequently Asked OBE [outcome-based evaluation] Questions," www.imls.gov/applicants/faqs.shtm.

29. Based on items including Nicolle O. Steffen, Keith Curry Lance, and Rochelle Logan, "Time to Tell the Whole Story: Outcome-Based Evaluation and the Counting on Results Project" (part one), *Public Libraries* 41, no. 4 (July/August 2002): 222–28; Nicolle O. Steffen and Keith Curry Lance, "Who's Doing What: Outcome-Based Evaluation and Demographics in the Counting on Results Project" (part two), *Public Libraries* 41, no. 5 (September/October, 2002): 271–79; Rhea Joyce Rubin, *Demonstrating Results: Using Outcome Measurement in Your Library* (Chicago: ALA Editions, 2005).

30. Ken Blanchard and Sheldon Bowles, *Raving Fans: A Revolutionary Approach to Customer Service* (New York: William Morrow and Company, 1993).

31. Based on items including Glen E. Holt, "Determining the Value of Library Services," paper presented at the IMPACT 2000 LSTA State Programs Conference, Institute of Museum and Library Services, Washington, DC, November 2000, 3–7; Tom Storey, "Public Libraries Pack a Powerful $$$ Punch," *OCLC Newsletter*, no. 267 (January/February/March 2005): 13–14, www.oclc.org/news/publications/newsletters/oclc/2005/267/advocacy.htm.

32. *The 2003 OCLC Environmental Scan: Pattern Recognition* (Dublin, OH: OCLC Online Computer Library Center, Inc., 2003).

33. *Perceptions of Libraries and Information Resources*, 2005, part 6, "Conclusions" (Dublin, OH: OCLC Online Computer Library Center, Inc. 2005), 6-1 to 6-8.

34. *Perceptions of Libraries and Information Resources*, 2005, part 6, "Conclusions," 6-5.

35. *Perceptions of Libraries and Information Resources*, 2005, part 6, "Conclusions," 6-7.

36. R. Roosevelt Thomas Jr., *Building on the Promise of Diversity: How We Can Move to the Next Level in Our Workplaces, Our Communities, and Our Society* (New York: American Management Association, 2006): xi, 89, 91, 101.

37. Thomas, *Building on the Promise of Diversity*, 103.

38. Peter Senge, *The Fifth Discipline* (New York: Doubleday/Currency, 1990): 5–11.

39. Joan Giesecke and Beth MacNeil, "Transitioning to the Learning Organization," *Library Trends* 53, no. 1 (Summer 2004): 54–67.

40. Peter Senge, *Dance of Change* (New York: Currency/Doubleday, 1999).

41. Susan Annis Hammond, *The Thin Book of Appreciative Inquiry*, 2nd ed. (Plano, TX: Thin Book Publishing Co., 1998).

42. Maureen Sullivan, "The Promise of Appreciative Inquiry in Library Organizations," *Library Trends* 53, no. 1 (Summer 2004): 218–29.

43. Sullivan, "The Promise of Appreciative Inquiry," 218–29.

44. Sullivan, "The Promise of Appreciative Inquiry," 218–29.

45. Etienne Wenger, *Communities of Practice: Learning, Meaning and Identity* (New York: Cambridge University Press, 1998); Etienne Wenger, *Cultivating Communities of Practice: A Guide to Managing Knowledge* (Boston: Harvard Business School Press, 2002).

46. Jeff De Cagna, "Tending the Garden of Knowledge: A Look at Communities of Practice with Etienne Wenger [interview]," *Information Outlook* 5, no. 7 (July 2001): 6–12.

47. Richard P. Chait, William P. Ryan, and Barbara E. Taylor, *Governance as Leadership: Reframing the Work of Nonprofit Boards* (Hoboken, NJ: John Wiley & Sons, 2005), 45, 126–29.

48. John Carver, *Boards That Make a Difference*, 3rd ed. (San Francisco: Jossey-Bass, 2006), 186–87.

49. American Marketing Association, *Dictionary of Marketing Terms*, www.marketingpower.com/mg-dictionary-view1862.php.

50. Storey, "Public Libraries Pack a Powerful $$$ Punch," 6–8.

51. Patricia H. Fisher and Marseille M. Pride, *Blueprint for Your Library Marketing Plan* (Chicago: American Library Association, 2006), 113–24.

52. Based on items including Linda K. Wallace, *Libraries, Mission and Marketing* (Chicago: ALA Editions, 2003); Rikvah K. Sass, "Marketing the Worth of Your Library," *Library Journal* 127, no. 11 (June 14, 2002): 37–38; *Missouri Libraries Your Lifetime Connection: A Marketing Manual for Missouri Library Staff and Trustees* (Jefferson City: Missouri State Library, 2004), 5.

53. Gina Millsap, director, Topeka-Shawnee County (Kansas) Public Library, interview with authors, April 24, 2006.

54. Atchison (Kansas) Library, "By Laws of the Board of Director," Section III Meetings, posted on KANLIB-L Listserv, April 19, 2006.

55. American Library Trustee Association, *Sample of Members and Non-Members* (Chicago: ALA Office for Research and Statistics, 1997); Ellen G. Miller and Patricia H. Fisher, *Final Report on Trustees as Urban Players*, submitted to the Urban Libraries Council, March 16, 2006, Appendix A, "Final Trustee Survey Report," 19–25. Used with permission.

56. Based on items including David C. Miller, "Term Limits," *Ohio Libraries* 17, no. 2 (Spring 2004): 30; Barbara Mooney, "Trustee Term Limits?" *Ohio Libraries* 17, no. 3 (Summer 2004): 25.

57. Based on items including F. Warren McFarlan, "Working on Nonprofit Boards: Don't Assume the Shoe Fits," *Harvard Business Review* 77, no. 6 (November/December 1999): 65–66; Alice Korngold, *Leveraging Good Will: Strengthening Nonprofits by Engaging Businesses* (San Francisco: Jossey-Bass, 2005), 96–98.

58. "Recruiting Interview," *T3: Trustee Training Tips* 4, no. 4 (Winter 2003): 3.

59. Rose Mosley, trustee, Maywood (Illinois) Public Library District, e-mail to authors, May 4, 2006.

60. Donald Roalkvam, trustee, Indian Trails (Illinois) Public Library District, interview with and e-mail to authors, May 3, 2006.

61. Rosalind McGee, trustee, Salt Lake City (Utah) Public Library, e-mail to authors, May 1, 2006; also telephone interview, May 2, 2006.

62. Cynthia Berner-Harris, director, Wichita (Kansas) Public Library, e-mail to authors, May 4, 2006.

63. "Trustee Essential #27: Trustee Orientation and Continuing Education," http://dpi.wi.gov/pld/te27.html.

64. *Michigan Public Library Trustee Manual*, 2004 ed. (Lansing: Library of Michigan, 2004), 8–9, available only at www.michigan.gov/documents/hal_lm_trusteemanual 2004_107173_7.pdf.

65. "Building a Board Team," *T3: Trustee Training Tips* 5, no. 4 (Winter 2004): 2.

66. Chait, Ryan, and Taylor, *Governance as Leadership,* 167–72.

67. BoardSource, "Common Questions about the Self-Assessment of the Board," www.boardsource.org/Knowledge.asp?ID=1.349; "Self-Assessment for Nonprofit Governing Boards," www.boardsource.org/Knowledge.asp?ID=1.349; Thomas P. Holland and Myra Blackmon, *Measuring Board Effectiveness* (Washington, DC: BoardSource, 2000).

68. Dan Cain, "The Board Evaluation Kit," www.cain-consulting.com/board evaluation.html; Ken Haycock, "Effective Board Governance," www.kenhaycock .com/media/ppt/Boards_BoardEffectiveness.ppt; Jeff Hixon, *A Self-Assessment Process for Kansas Public Library Boards* (Lawrence: Northeast Kansas Library System, 2002).

69. "The Board Evaluates Itself," *IN the Public Trust* (Indianapolis, IN: State Library, 2003), B10–11; "Self-Evaluation for Trustees," *Georgia Public Library Trustees Handbook,* 2nd ed. (Birmingham: Public Library Services Georgia Department of Education, 1995), 142–43.

70. Based on items including Marion Peters Angelica, "Resolving Board Conflicts." Google "Marion Peters Angelica," then click the title to get the pdf file; Marion Peters Angelica, *Resolving Conflict in Nonprofit Organizations* (St. Paul, MN: Amherst H. Wilder Foundation, 1999), 114–16; Marion Peters Angelica, *Keeping the Peace: Resolving Conflict in the Boardroom* (Washington, DC: National Center for Nonprofit Boards, 2000), 14–15.

71. Daniel L. Kurtz and Sarah E. Paul, *Managing Conflicts of Interest: A Primer for Nonprofit Boards,* 2nd ed. (Washington, DC: BoardSource, 2006).

72. Linda J. Dawson and Randy Quinn, "Why Board Culture Matters," *American School Board Journal* 191, no. 9 (September 2004): 28–31.

73. "Trustee Censured for Removing Newspapers," *American Libraries* 34, no. 9 (October 2003): 10–11; "Libertyville Renews Ethics Policy, Despite Challenges," American Libraries 35, no. 3 (March 2004): 17.

74. Jan Masaoka, "Removing a Difficult Board Member," in *The Best of the Board Café* (St. Paul, MN: Wilder Publishing Center, 2003), 109.

CHAPTER 4

Getting and Growing the Funding Your Library Needs

Quick View

No matter how math-challenged some trustees may be, most get the basics when it comes to library revenues and expenditures:

- They scan monthly budget reports, comparing this year to the previous two.
- They look for large increases and decreases in line items or programs.
- They understand how a home's market value (say, $200,000) has a fractional assessed value (such as 10 percent, or $20,000) that is applied to the library levy (of, say, 4.5 mills, or $.0045), resulting in property tax revenue to the library (in this case, $90.00).

What may be missing? Realizing that carrying out their fiduciary responsibility to obtain needed revenues takes the entire director-board team, not just the director and a couple of trustee number wonks. The team's job is to obtain all possible levies and other funds, prepare and monitor budgets, watch out for tax abatements that could cut library revenue, and advocate effectively for needed funds. Having community leaders on the board helps in these important jobs.

Public dollar revenue dominates this chapter for three reasons:

1. *Major source.* Most libraries get the vast majority of their revenue from public dollars such as property (ad valorem, meaning based on value or worth) and other taxes, the local government's general

fund, special levies, transfers, grants, and voted debt.

2. *Variable legal powers*. Boards with full governing powers do it all—set levies and approve budgets. Partial governing boards must get money or budget approval from the city, county, or other local government unit. Advisory boards have few or no legal powers over either the levy or budgets.

   However, all boards regardless of their legal powers have a responsibility to advocate for the maximum in public dollars.

3. *Curbs on library revenues*. State or local governments might unilaterally cut library revenues through tax abatements and credits lasting for ten, twenty, or even more years.

The following topics are covered in this chapter:

- Revenue from public dollars
- Revenue from private dollars
- Curbs on getting public dollars
- Advocacy that protects or gets dollars
- Chapter checkup: "Next Agenda Item: Tax Abatement Update" (See the website for answers to the chapter check up.)

Sidebar 4.1.
Library Financial Definitions

Terminology means everything when it comes to library financial management. Start with this common-sense list of major terms, then get local details from your director, local government, or state library.

Assessed valuation (property or ad valorem taxes). **A small percentage of a property's market value as appraised by local government. Example: A house worth $200,000 is assessed at 10 percent of that value, or $20,000.**

Budgets. **An itemized list of expected revenues and expenditures. Revenue examples of public dollars include items such as ad valorem (real property), motor vehicle, and sales taxes. Other sources often include interest on investments, fees and fines, carryovers from previous fiscal year, gifts, and grants. Expenditure examples: The operational budget typically includes all personnel expenses, collections, and technology. The special use budget often includes other items such as debt service, capital expenditures, and general maintenance.**

Capital improvements budget. **See Budgets.**

Carryover. **At the end of a fiscal year, the unspent dollars and unanticipated revenues that remain in library funds and that may be carried over to the next fiscal year's budget, per the budget process or applicable laws.**

Debt service. **The dollars allocated annually to pay off debt that voters approved or debt that is allowed by statute. Example: A $22 million bond issue for a new branch library has a twenty-year amortization period, resulting in a debt service expenditure for twenty years.**

As explained in the preface, check this book's companion website (www .pfisherassociates.com/scarecrow-press/sources.html) to download adaptable forms and answers to the chapter checkup quiz. Also see the website for additional sources. One caveat for financial professionals: Technical terms may be used in a common sense way. For the authors' intent, see the sidebar 4.1.

Revenue from Public Dollars

Is the glass half full or half empty for funding the nation's 9,214 public libraries? The nearly $9 billion spent in 2003 isn't exactly pocket change. See the National Center for Education Statistics' breakdown, shown in table 4.1.

As shown in table 4.1, local government contributed the lion's share. Private dollars came from the Friends of the Library, library foundations, donors, partnerships, and others. Another analysis by the National Commission on Libraries and Information Science showed a $3.5 billion increase in library funding between 1992 and 2002.[1]

How stable is library funding? Overall for fiscal years 2003, 2004, and 2005, not bad. Between 77 percent and 82 percent of the 468 public libraries participating in an American Library Association (ALA) study reported level

Sidebar 4.1.
(continued)

Dedicated library levy. A dedicated percentage of property, sales, and other taxes that goes to the library. Usually voted by a public referendum, it may have been authorized by vote of an elected body.

Expenditures. Itemized categories of permitted expenses. See Budgets for sample categories.

General funds allocation. The amount received by the library from city, township, or county common funds after competition with the police, parks and recreation, and other entities.

Funds. The legally permitted holding bins for revenue received. Examples: general, capital improvements, gifts, debt service.

Line item. An individual category of expense, such as salaries, wages, personnel benefits, utilities, vehicles, and so on.

Mill levy. The percentage that a library is able to charge against assessed values. However, due to state or local laws, some libraries even with full governing powers cannot exceed a levy cap without a public vote. The levy is expressed in mills, meaning one-tenth of a cent, or .001 of a dollar. Example: 2.5 mills would be expressed as .0025; for the house with $20,000 assessed value it would yield $50.00.

Operational budget. See Budgets.

Referendum. A vote by the public at special, local, or general elections. Some states, such as Michigan, require referenda (the plural) on both operational and capital budgets.

Revenue. Income to the library from diverse sources. See Budgets for typical public and private sources.

Transfers. Permitted movement of dollars from one fund, budget, or line item to another during a fiscal year.

Table 4.1. National Breakdown of Source of Public Library Funds, 2003

Source	Type	Amount	Percent of Grand Total
Federal funds	Public	$48,152,364	.5 percent
State funds	Public	$951,953,624	10.9 percent
Local funds (city, county, township, other)	Public	$6,991,601,628	80 percent
Total public		$7,991,707,616	91.4 percent
Donors, Friends, and so on	Private	$752,295,458	8.6 percent
Grand total		$8,744,003,074	100 percent

funding in each of those years. Is that good news? No, since flat funding doesn't handle population growth or personnel, book, utility, and other costs.[2]

Revenue from Public Dollars

Getting a grip on public dollars received by libraries is like untangling a vat of spaghetti Alfredo: messy but doable.

Start by comparing your library's revenue sources with those shown in figure 4.1. Which taxes, special levies, transfers, capital bonds (voted debt), federal funds, and reimbursements does your library get? Could it get under state law?

Alert: Do use terms correctly. During the board meeting, a trustee may erroneously say "taxes" when in fact the revenue comes from fees or reimbursements. That goof will likely raise eyebrows of business leaders when reported in tomorrow's newspaper.

Property and Other Taxes

Director-board team, which tax demands constant attention? The property (ad valorem) tax. It is not only your library's largest single revenue source, but also visible and controversial for Tina and Tony Taxpayer.

Taxes

	Local Taxes	State Taxes
Tangible (real estate) property	√	√
Intangible (personal) property	√	√
Sales	√	√
Income/earnings	√	√
Excise and transfer	√	√
Delinquent	√	√

Special Levies/Funds Allowed
(Example from State of Illinois)

- Audit fund
- State retirement fund
- Medicare/Social Security (FICA) fund
- Building/maintenance fund
- Insurance fund for buildings, liability, and errors and omissions (but not health)

Transfers/Grants/Reimbursements from Other Public Entities

State library, for example, special projects, interlibrary loan
Regional/cooperative library systems
City
County
Township
School district
Pro rata costs, for example, hosting or creating databases, digitization, and so on

Capital Bonds (Voted Debt)

Purposes

Facilities (construction or remodeling)
Technology; other equipment (e.g., HVAC)
Land

Federal Funds

Library Services and Technology Act (LSTA) via state library
Direct grants, for example, congressional projects; Institute for Museum and Library Services (IMLS) for native Americans

Figure 4.1.   Examples of Public Dollars That Libraries Might Receive

Other eyes watch property taxes, too, such as tax-cutter groups and the media. Their spotlights provide a golden opportunity for your team. Show how the library delivers benefits to taxpayers. Provide an ongoing stream of talk radio and luncheon gigs, billboards, blogs (weblogs, part of many library websites), website updates, articles, and more to demonstrate how your library uses their tax dollars to make a difference in your community.

Other taxes received may include retail sales tax on items ranging from ice cream cones to RVs (recreational vehicles). One pesky item: delinquent taxes and those under appeal, which short the current fiscal year but unexpectedly aid a future fiscal year. Make sure your library gets an annual allocation of delinquent taxes received rather than waiting for several years for a large lump sum.

Aside from taxes, other public dollars, as shown in figure 4.1, might include special levies, transfers, capital bonds (voted debt), federal funds, and reimbursements.

Special Levies

Given the contentious nature of property (ad valorem) taxes, look for ways to reduce your library's dependence on them. By state or local law, some libraries are empowered to set special tax levies, thereby relieving the operating levy. For example, Illinois permits several separate levies and resulting funds such as the following (ILCS stands for Illinois Compiled Statutes):

- Audit Fund only for the library's annual audit expenses (65 ILCS 5/8-8-8)
- Illinois Municipal Retirement Fund (40 ILCS 5/7-171)
- Medicare/Social Security Fund, only for FICA expenses (40 ILCS 5/21-110 and 21-110.1)
- Building/Maintenance Fund for items such as purchase of sites and building; rental; maintenance, repair, and alterations (75ILCS 5/3-1 and 75 ILCS 16/356-10)
- Insurance Fund, but only for building, liability, and "errors and omissions" insurances, not for health insurance costs (745 ILCS 10/9-107).[3] For details on insurances, see chapter 1.

In Kansas, an employee benefit levy for libraries is permitted under KSA 12-16, 102 (KSA stands for Kansas Statutes Annotated). The library board passes a resolution that shows up in its minutes. Then the director and perhaps some board members go to the municipality seeking action; it is active upon publication. A Kansas attorney general's opinion stated that once in place, the employee benefit levy cannot be abolished.[4]

Excise and transfer taxes cover all real estate transactions and are usually targeted for infrastructure such as roads and school construction. Washington County, Maryland, provides some funds from this source for library renovation and construction.[5]

Grants

The leading example in most states is the state aid grant made to each local library. A 2003 national comparison of public library standards showed that of the twenty-eight responding states, only Vermont and New Hampshire provided no state aid.[6]

Nationally, state aid purposes vary tremendously, from per capita payments to funds for special programs or groups. Often, the legislature may cut or increase it. In Pennsylvania, the FY2003/2004 state aid of $75.3 million was severely cut in FY2004/2005, but funds were restored to $61.3 million in FY2005/2006.

Most state aid is linked to voluntary or legal requirements, such as numbers of hours open and director's qualifications. For many small public libraries, state aid is invaluable, paying for all new materials and many daily costs. In Pennsylvania, on average it provides about 16–18 percent of public library income.[7]

Regional library groups may provide grants, too. Several states, such as Texas, New York, California, Illinois, New Jersey, Florida, Kansas, Indiana, and Massachusetts, have regional systems, groups, or cooperative library organizations. Some serve only members; others address just a single type of library (e.g., public). Still others serve only libraries in a geographic area. Regional groups' services may include purchasing pools, library board training, and sending out computer- and bookmobiles.[8]

Some regional library groups offer grants to their local public libraries; those that support a state's trustee organization are of special interest. For example, the Northeast Kansas Library System, covering fourteen counties, has an eight-tiered system of grant criteria. The top four tiers require institutional membership in the Kansas Library Trustee Association and its parent Kansas Library Association. For FY2007, the grants for those top four tiers ranged from $18,000 for a Major Service Center I to $51,550 for a Major Resource Library.[9]

Transfers and Reimbursements

Libraries often provide services to other entities. Local schools, courts, and others may transfer funds to the library to house literacy offices and classrooms or provide materials and staffing for outreach in juvenile courts.

A state library may provide reimbursements for handling interlibrary loan requests, with extra funds going to those libraries loaning substantially more than they request. Or a library may receive its prorated costs for cooperative projects such as digitizing fragile documents or creating a shared database of state historical materials.

Voted Debt

Voted debt for capital expenditures covers items such as library facilities, technology, equipment, and land. Sometimes the library board, city council, county commission, or other legally authorized entity approves the capital project.

But even when a governmental entity has the legal power to OK your $2 million remodeling project, it may defer to a public vote, thereby avoiding criticism for a possibly controversial decision. Historically, library referenda have been favorably received. Table 1.2 in chapter 1 shows over two-thirds of the building issues approved annually.

Federal Funds

Federal dollars reach many public libraries, whether directly or indirectly. The two most familiar programs are the Library Services and Technology

Act (LSTA) and e-rate (discounts offered to public libraries under the Telecommunications Act of 1996). Chapter 1 discusses in depth how libraries seeking LSTA or e-rate funds must, according to the Children's Internet Protection Act, filter all Web-connected computers, a step taken by an estimated 40 percent of the nation's libraries.

LSTA funding is provided to each state library by the Institute for Museum and Library Services (IMLS). State libraries often use LSTA dollars for statewide purposes such as licensing databases or software. Some also offer individual grants to local libraries. IMLS also provides grants for special populations. For example, the Blackfeet Tribe of Browning, Montana, received a $6,000 Native American Library Services Grant in 2006.

E-rate discounts range from 20 percent to 90 percent for telecommunications services, Internet access, and closely related costs such as inside wiring. The greater a community's need, the larger the discount, which totals about $2.25 billion per year nationally. Despite controversy over alleged fraud and abuse, grassroots library advocacy with Congress assured that the program continues.[10]

Are other federal funds available to libraries? Yes. One program for rural America deserves note. Libraries in rural communities meeting poverty and other needs indicators have used Community Facilities Loans and Grants available from the U.S. Department of Agriculture's Rural Development housing and community programs. Its website includes libraries under the category of "public services," along with city halls, homeless shelters, and street improvement. For example, a joint city hall–public library renovation project in Burns, Kansas, utilized a $50,000 loan and a $50,000 grant from Rural Development, along with $90,000 in local funding.[11]

Director-board team, get relief for that old warhorse, the property tax, which is the basis for the general fund allotment. Obtain as many other types of public dollars as possible.

Making Money from Public Dollars

It's one thing to have a diverse stream of public dollars. It's another to make money from it. Two methods, investments and sale of surplus property, are typically authorized by a state.

Investments

Public dollars tend to come in two or three installments annually, resulting in an opportunity to make extra money by investing dollars not needed for several weeks or months.

Investment powers and practices of library boards vary hugely. State and local laws, as well as the library's bylaws and regulations, help define interest-earning opportunities. Typically they set stringent limits on investments.

The goal? Low to no risk of losing public dollars. That means avoiding the situation of one California public library that invested nearly all of its trust fund in utility and energy companies. During the energy bust of the early 2000s, it lost nearly $100,000 in stocks that had been donated years before. The board felt that it would weather the bear market, but a local financial planner criticized the portfolio for not having a stated goal such as building a new library.[12]

In Indiana, boards have the legal authority per Indiana Code 5-13-9-1 to handle their own investments; purchasing securities on margin, such as the stock market, is forbidden. Approved vehicles per Indiana Code 5-13-9-2(a)(2) include U.S. government securities, repurchase agreements, money market mutual funds, bonds with specific ratings, sweep accounts, savings accounts, and CDs (certificates of deposit).

Indiana's Plainfield-Guilford Township Public Library reported good results through a low-interest state loan via a tax anticipation warrant program. The loan is available to any unit needing to even out its cash flow. "Since we get distributions twice a year, there are predictably a couple of months each year when we need to have this borrowed cash available," stated director Charr Skirvin. "But until we need the cash, we invest the loan by purchasing a CD or putting it in a high-interest savings account."[13]

Georgia statute 36-83-4 permits investments or reinvestments in items such as State of Georgia and U.S. government obligations, prime bankers' acceptances, and local government investment pools. It states that "in selecting among avenues of investment or among institutional bids for deposits, the highest rate of return shall be the objective, given equivalent conditions of safety and liquidity."[14]

How much visibility should investment income get? Supporters see it as demonstrating the leadership team's financial acumen. More money earned means more programs and services can benefit families, seniors, homeschoolers, and other stakeholders.

But critics may see earned income as a reason to try to reduce public funds by an equal amount. If, for example, the library earned $20,000 in interest, some argue that the library's general allocation from the city or county should be reduced by that amount. Preventing such budget cuts is one reason why state standards may require local public dollars to stay at the same level to assure continued state-aid grants.

For example, Oklahoma's Rules and Regulations for State Aid Grants to Public Libraries state that "Local government must continue to expend an amount for library service, i.e., operating expenditures, not less than that of the preceding fiscal year" (maintenance of local effort).[15]

Sale of Public Property

Many libraries are permitted to sell surplus public property such as land, buildings, and equipment. Controversy may arise when opinions differ as to what is "surplus." Be sure to have excellent documentation about the library's ownership of those nineteenth-century landscapes or rare books before contacting Sotheby's or Christie's.

Team, do your homework before auctioning intangible items such as naming rights. The Womelsdorf (Pennsylvania) Community Library needed funds to complete part of an expansion project. Its first eBay auction attracted one bid for $325,000, down $50,000 from the reserve price. The second time, no one bid.[16]

It's one thing to list types of possible public dollars your library might get. It's another to actually deposit them in the bank.

Dedicated versus Local General Fund Revenue

For many libraries, securing needed public dollars means competition. Annually, they go up against the police, parks department, and other local entities for local general fund allocations.

For those general fund libraries, the property tax goes into the city or county general fund. The library may get only 1 percent or 1.5 percent of the entire fund. It's essential to watch that percentage closely each year and in relationship to other public services. Is the library's piece of that general fund pie increasing, staying flat, or decreasing?

Other libraries benefit from a dedicated tax for the library's exclusive use. Urban Libraries Council (ULC) members serve populations over 100,000. In one study of ninety-six ULC members, sixty-eight (or 70.8 percent) reported using local dedicated property, sales, or other taxes. Another forty-seven (or 48.6 percent) reported using local general funds. Eight reported using both dedicated taxes and general funds.[17]

Another national study sponsored by the Public Library Association looked at all public libraries regardless of the size of population served. Barely one-fourth of them had independent taxing authority. That left a whopping three-fourths dependent on money allocated by a local government from the general fund. Of the 926 U.S. responding libraries, 23.54 percent (or 218 libraries) reported having independent taxing authority. In comparison with the ULC study, only 4 (or 16 percent) of the largest libraries, serving 1 million population or more, reported having an independent taxing authority. Further research is needed.[18]

Public libraries seeking allocations from the local general fund are up against some tough competition, especially concerning public safety, public health, and environmental issues. If the police need three new patrol cars, it's easy for your library's allocation to be cut by $90,000. There goes the money intended for foreign-language audio books.

It takes time and dollars for the library's board-director team to make its case. Presentations to city council and schmoozing with the county commissioners may last for weeks. Worse, this year's hard work and success get repeated next year.

Another important consideration about the local government's general fund is the categories of agencies it has. If the categories are Recreation and Parks, Education, Public Safety, and others, the library wants to be in a category that is ranked high in priority when it comes to the quality of life of the citizens. That's why Mary Baykan, director of the

Washington County (Maryland) Public Library, helped move her library from the nonprofits/charities portion of the county's general fund pool into the education category. "I wanted us to be seen as an educational function, not as a non-essential service," Baykan said. "By being labeled 'education,' we get taken more seriously and are given more consideration at budget time." Baykan showed county officials the Public Library Law that states that "public library resources and services are essential components of the educational system."[19]

Why set up a dedicated library levy or become an independent taxing authority? To guard against revenue fluctuations that can cut services to stakeholders. It also saves your director-board team time and dollars otherwise spent in annual competition with other governmental units.

No matter whether your library has a dedicated levy or competes for an allotment from the general fund, stakeholders want to see ROI (return on investment) from their public dollars. Taxpayers, officials, property owners, civic and business leaders, and the media seek library accountability, which starts by gathering opinions from those who use library services. Publicize those outcomes, discussed in chapter 3, through your library's own annual report, website, and blogs; speaking gigs at leadership groups; regular contacts with city and county officials; and media coverage.

Accountability in a public entity begins with its management of public dollars. Who makes those decisions for libraries? The director-board team, captained by your director.

The Revenue Management Team

Whether your library has a dedicated levy or competes for general revenue dollars, the buck stops with your director. Even with a budget manager and a knowledgeable board finance committee, the director must know the library's overall financial position at all times and report it regularly to the board. Unlike the CEOs of scandal-ridden Enron or Tyco, library heads cannot plead ignorance of what underlings were doing.

Some library boards have a finance committee. Typical responsibilities carried out in conjunction with the director include the following:

- Preparing draft operational and capital budgets, including revenue and expense, for board review
- Identifying upcoming capital expenses that will require obtaining new funds
- Working with the board's auditor

Sometimes the finance committee proposes more than just the operating budget. For example, the Kansas City (Missouri) Public Library's Finance & Budget Committee recommended to the full board adopting five budgets for FY2005/2006—Library Operating Budget, Gifts/Grants Fund Budget, Capital Development Fund Budget, LSTA Fund Budget, and Enterprise Fund Budget.[20] If there is no budget director, the finance committee chairperson in conjunction with the director usually presents regular reports at board meetings.

Revenue from Private Dollars

No matter how many public dollars a library receives, there rarely are enough to carry out the library's strategic plan. Many libraries turn to private dollars. However, opinions vary on that practice. In a point-counterpoint discussion, Steve Coffman supported plural funding that mixes public and private dollars, while Thomas Hennen urged holding local officials accountable for full funding of public dollars.[21]

In reality, most libraries seek and get private dollars with the blessing of state or local laws and their own bylaws. For example, New Jersey tells its trustees that "financing of public libraries is addressed in this manual because assuring adequate funds for library services is a prime responsibility of trustees. . . . It is essential that trustees are knowledgeable about available financing methods: local taxes and appropriations, fines, gifts and bequests, special purpose allocations, grants, federal funds, capital funds, State Aid, and building support funds."[22] The goal is receiving the maximum funds possible.

Attracting Private Dollars

For decades, libraries have used self-help methods to earn extra money. The ULC's report on ninety-six members showed how many libraries received money from entrepreneurial efforts and private sources. See table 4.2.[23]

The iconic fund-raising methods are used book sales and "dinner in the stacks" galas. The online book sale, one of several newer methods, claims to earn money for libraries while saving staff time and storage space. To test the cost and benefits of using a vendor to sell library discards via an online auction, the Baltimore County Public Library decided to try three shipments of pallets of boxed, used books to a commercial firm. That firm then listed the books with an online vendor such as eBay, Amazon, or Barnes & Noble. The firm's tasks included receiving, sorting, pricing, listing, storing, picking, packing, and shipping sold items. The library's task was to sort and process books at sixteen branches, move them to a central site, and shrink-wrap the pallets so they could be shipped. At the end of the test, it was decided that this method was not cost effective for a library system with many branches.[24]

On the positive side, entrepreneurial efforts do much more than make money. The library's coffee shop and bookstore are image setters.

Table 4.2. Entrepreneurial and Private Source Funds of Urban Library Council Members

Source	Number	Percent
Entrepreneurial efforts		
Bookstores	22	23 percent
Space rental/lease	34	35 percent
Coffee shop	19	20 percent
Private sources		
Gifts from individuals	73	76 percent
Gifts from corporations	62	65 percent
Gifts from foundations	65	68 percent
Friends of the library groups	74	77 percent

Food, merchandise with the library's logo, affordable books—all help show the community that it's not just "your grandpa's library."

On the downside, entrepreneurial efforts take dollars, time, and space away from other library activities. Even when these efforts are staffed by volunteers, supervision is needed. These costs help explain the lure of fund-raising, whose goal is getting dollars, not making retail sales.

Historically, the individual donor has been the bedrock of library fund-raising. Large or small, donations add up. They also help build relationships, showing the donor's friends that the library is a worthy cause to aid.

Some libraries seek "now" gifts for immediate purposes. They include the ubiquitous summer reading programs as well as minor facilities upgrades and ongoing operational expenses. The ULC survey showed private funding of operational budgets ranging from 40 percent for Providence (Rhode Island) Public Library to several in the 5–10 percent range, including Boston, Brooklyn, Denver, Enoch Pratt, and others. The Kansas City (Missouri) Public Library strives for 10 percent of its operational costs to be supported by private dollars.[25]

Others go for "later" gifts such as endowments, bequests, and other estate-planning devices. The goal is capital acquisition whose interest may be spent in the future.

The workhorse organizations? Friends of the Library or the library's own foundation. Their main tool? 501(c)3 IRS (Internal Revenue Service) status. In the traditional division of labor, Friends go after smaller, "now" gifts, while the foundation pursues larger, "later" donations.

Assuming appropriate state laws, a 501(c)3 may offer financial leverage to the library as well as tax exemptions to the donor. For example, in Ohio a couple donated $250,000 to the Fairfield County District Library's foundation, which built and held title to the branch building. Leasing the building back to the library provided the foundation with income; it then mortgaged the building to provide additional money to construct a second branch.[26]

Seeking Large Donations

This discussion, while recognizing the political and cumulative financial importance of low-dollar donors, emphasizes large infusions of private dollars. Of course, "large" depends on the library's circumstances. Fifty thousand dollars, large for a library with a $4 million operational budget and no foundation, is minor for the library with a $43 million operational budget and a generous Friends group.

Fortunately, the extensive library literature on fund-raising targets all sizes of libraries and, by implication, all three types of library boards.[27] The nonprofit literature is also abundant and helpful. It includes hardcopy and electronic versions of who's who in the nation's top 20,000 foundations, including subject field.[28]

For the interested director-board team, an outside speaker could provide timely tips and facts. And on nights when you can't sleep, Googling "public library fundraising" results in over 1 million hits to peruse.

Cause Marketing

One newer fund-raising method is cause marketing. It marries business marketing with a nonprofit's good cause to financially benefit each. Cause marketing allies a corporate brand with a nonprofit entity's socially important purpose in a strategic, collaborative relationship to "create shareholder and social value and to publicly communicate values."[29]

Examples include American Express supporting a campaign to raise money to restore the Statue of Liberty. It donated one cent to that cause for every use of its credit cards. Card usage went up 28 percent. New card holders totaled 45 percent. Successful cause-marketing programs have four central themes, wrote Jocelyn Daw:

1. "Partner: Strategic intersection of societal needs and corporate goals." It pairs two entities that create a strategic, mutually beneficial collaboration. Each advances the other's agenda while sharing responsibilities, contributions, and risks.
2. "Purpose: Value exchange plus philanthropy." Cause marketing goes past traditional corporate philanthropy or sponsorship. "To be successful, nonprofits must think like businesses and understand their needs and objectives. They must recognize the valuable assets they can bring, including their brand, reputation, community linkages, and networks and programs."

3. "Passion: Making a difference by combining assets and strengths.
   . . . Cause marketing creates synergies by building on strengths and
   assets of each partner, making the sum of the two parts greater than
   each individual part."

4. "Profits: Mutual benefit to create value, communicate values. . . .
   Each element builds on the others, with the ultimate results being
   value creation and value reflection for the corporation, nonprofit
   organization and in the end stakeholders engaged in supporting
   and participating in cause-marketing programs."[30]

Implementation includes developing the project, market, and target
markets; showing benefits to both parties to the proposed partner; creating a timeline; and providing the partner with many visibility opportunities. Examples include Lance Armstrong's "Livestrong" and the breast
cancer "Spread Beauty. Share Hope" bracelets.

Some libraries have used cause-related marketing. "We're not selling
wristbands, we're selling our causes," opined Illinois' Alliance Library
System, which advertised a retail price of $3 per bracelet. However, some
look askance at cause marketing because brand images can drop. Today's
favorite breakfast cereal may be next year's dog. The Foundation Center
notes that one common criticism is that nonprofits might modify existing
programs merely to attract cause-related marketing dollars. Another worry
is that only noncontroversial causes would be chosen.[31]

In their quest to attract more private dollars, some libraries are taking
advantage of another important source: baby boomer estates.

Historic Wealth Transfer

Family foundations. Community foundations. Nonprofit group leaders.
Professional fund-raisers. Estate planners. Acquaintances and friends.

Many hands eagerly help aging boomers transfer wealth from themselves to the next generation and to causes. The 1999 report *Millionaires
and the Millennium: New Estimates of the Forthcoming Wealth Transfer and
the Prospects for a Golden Age of Philanthropy* looked at the value of

78,839,311 estates to be left by boomers. It posited three scenarios, the most conservative being a $40.6 trillion transfer between 1998 and 2052. The breakdown showed estate fees at $1.6 trillion, estate taxes at $8.5 trillion, bequests to heirs $24.6 trillion, and bequests to charity $6 trillion. The $40.6 trillion estimate, despite the dot-com bust of the early 2000s, was upheld in a 2003 reanalysis by the authors of the 1999 report.

Others saw problems. While the 1999 report said that at least $1.7 trillion in bequests would be made to charities in the first twenty years, only $127.6 billion was actually bequeathed—just 7.5 percent of the expected amount. However, the report's authors stuck to their predictions, saying that they could occur later than expected.

Whether the transfer occurs sooner or later, libraries are busy seeking their fair share. "There is currently a huge transfer of wealth from one generation to the next that has tremendous potential for all charitable organizations," said Peter Pearson, president of the Friends of the St. Paul (Minnesota) Public Library. Susan Randolph saw the wealth transfer as a perfect time for public libraries with a little fundraising experience to focus on bequests.[32]

In addition to well-heeled boomers, many libraries target foundations, corporate donors, and partnerships. What do all those potential funders have in common? The need to see results. Whether it's improving lives, gaining access to desired markets, heightened visibility, or leaving a legacy, donors need to be shown how their dollars or in-kind contributions made a difference. Libraries, Friends, and library foundations seeking donor support must have the tools to measure and report on outcomes; see chapter 3 for details on outcome-based evaluation.

Preparing for Funders

Whichever donors you have targeted—individual, business, foundation, partnership, or more—you're not in the money-raising business at all. Instead, you're building relationships. Fund-raisers are important, but friend-raisers count more because they position the library as a worthy repository. Building those friendly relations requires a philosophy, a game plan, and ongoing commitment. Do remember that those relations rest on one essential action: You have to ask.

One must-have team tool? Policies that spell out what kinds of donors the library may seek. Examples of needed donor policies include the following:

- *Gifts*—spell out how all gifts, from books to property, are handled; see also chapter 1.
- *Third-party fund-raising*—state the circumstances under which an outside organization or person may raise money for the library. If you use this method, what are a project's criteria and library support?
- *Sponsorships*—specify the criteria for candidate organizations; see chapter 3.
- *Fund-raising ethics*—adopt clear statements prohibiting conflict of interest and personal benefit for outsiders soliciting on behalf of the library. Do include the library's commitment to spend money on the cause for which it was raised.
- *Solicitation*—list the acceptable types of fund-raising, such as gala events. Also designate the person or group having authority to approve proposed practices.
- *Donor recognition*—specify who gets it and how.[33]

Donor visibility gets special attention. The cardinal rule? Find out how much of it they want. Even "Anonymous" can be included in press releases and annual reports. For those donors who welcome visibility, start with press releases, photo ops, and in-person thanks at library and civic events. Also use your website, annual report, and celebratory events to point out each donor, and the amount or range donated.

For example, the Springfield-Greene County (Missouri) Library lists donors on its architecturally striking Wall of Honor in the central library foyer. Its website also shows snapshots of donated library facilities and collections, with the donors' names. At the 2006 ALA Midwinter meetings in San Antonio, we noted that the San Antonio Public Library puts signage with donor names on the ends of the stacks as well as listing them by size of gift on the foundation's website.

Director-board teams, you likely depend on both public and private dollars. But when it comes to those public funds, how much you actually get depends in part on the barriers permitted outsiders by law.

Curbs on Getting Public Dollars

The theory of legal checks and balances applies to public libraries. Most states grant powers to citizens and to local governmental entities that can reduce public revenues. The two examples discussed here are citizen powers and the unilateral steps that a city, county, or other jurisdiction may take.

Citizen Powers

Referenda and protest petitions are two common citizen curbs on library levies and budgets. The referenda's purpose is to permit yes-no decisions by those most affected: the taxpayers. Many states require referenda for capital budgets; some also require them for annual operational budgets. Some states, such as Michigan and New York, require both of those referenda. Historically, about two-thirds of all referenda pass, as chapter 1 noted.

Protest petitions let citizens try to block approval of a library budget or levy. For example, Hoosiers may protest at two major points.

First, before the budget is adopted. Ten or more taxpayers may file an objection petition with an Indiana library board within seven days of the public hearing on the library's budget. The petition must specifically identify the provisions of the budget, tax rate, and tax levy to which the taxpayers object.

If citizens object in writing, the board must respond and file a copy with the county auditor of that response with the official budget paperwork. The library board doesn't have to accept the objections or change its budget (Indiana Code 6-1.1-17-5(b)).

Second, after the budget has been adopted. Upon receipt of the adopted library budget, the county auditor advertises all property tax rates of all political subdivisions. At that point, ten or more taxpayers may file a statement of appeal, specifying the provisions of the budget and tax levy to which they object. However, 75 percent of those ten or more taxpayers must have signed the earlier "before" petition (IC 6-1.1-17-13(b)).

The postadoption appeal ends up at the Indiana Department of Local Government Finance. Historically, about 99 percent of the postadoption library appeals have resulted in the department upholding the library.[34]

For details about citizen protests under your state and local laws or library bylaws, see your director. While likely an infrequent occurrence, citizen petitions may be accompanied with visibility that gets your library on local talk radio and in the paper.

Local Government Powers

Remember driving in pea-soup fog? Low to no visibility also applies to the many curbs that local governments might place on library revenues. City, county, and township decisions about tax abatements or credits, taken with or without the library board's knowledge, could result in lowered revenue estimates, mid-fiscal-year adjustments, or rescheduling capital improvements.

Tax Abatements and Credits

Virtually all cities and counties seek economic development. That means attracting new businesses or helping local business expand, adding jobs and businesses that grow the tax base. The resulting higher income, sales, and property taxes get shared among schools, libraries, police, parks and recreation, and other qualifying local entities. Their actions helping economic development not only bring in more revenue but also help position the individuals involved as part of the community's leadership team, as discussed in chapter 5.

Two major economic carrots help local government attract businesses and development. *Tax credits* permit an entity to deduct amounts from taxes owed. *Tax abatements* don't levy the tax in the first place.

Companies and developers seek the incentives as a way to reduce their costs, usually pitting one jurisdiction against another. The winning state, city, or county trumpets the benefits of new jobs, spending, and taxes.

But these carrots come with a big flaw: lost revenue to public entities such as library, school, and other special districts. Property (ad valorem) taxes provide the majority of revenue for libraries either through a dedicated library levy or as the basis of the general fund from which the library gets an allotment. Because they are a key financial source, abatements that decrease the yield from property taxes are emphasized in this chapter. They provide full or partial tax relief, thereby either reducing the cost of, or providing funds for, economic development or redevelopment. Nationally, their popularity has grown dramatically since World War II.

In 1964, fifteen states offered property tax abatements; by 2005, thirty-five did. States vary in whether the abatement is granted for land, improvements to the land, commercial property, or personal property. Fifteen states had only one tax abatement program, whereas Minnesota had six, and Maryland had seven.[35]

Tax Increment Financing

In addition to the thirty-five state programs, most cities, counties, townships, and other local jurisdictions offer tax abatements, such as tax increment financing (TIF). Its intent is to help blighted, difficult-to-develop properties. TIF lets developers and businesses use a project's increased tax revenues to pay for permitted items such as land, facilities, and equipment.

For example, Indiana specifies that buildings, manufacturing equipment, research, and development equipment may be abated. In Missouri, the current TIF laws have been criticized for misuse that permits developers to turn vacant agricultural land into shopping malls; attempts have been made to define "blight" much more carefully to include items such as dilapidation, inadequate utilities, and environmental cleanup.[36]

The outcome? Higher tax value for the property. However, taxing entities such as cities, counties, school districts, and libraries cannot reap revenues based on the higher tax value until the TIF expires, which may be ten, twenty, or more years.

Dollars versus principles. What's the impact of TIFs on public libraries? It depends. The revenue loss to libraries due to tax abatements can be numerically small. For example, in FY2006, the Johnson County (Kansas) Library showed $125,614 in Library General TIF (tax increment funds), or .007 percent of the $18,214,428 operating fund. Its $26,253 in Special Use Fund TIF was also .007 percent of that $3,400,379 budget.[37]

The Portage (Michigan) District Library shared a loss of $21,000 with four other entities when city council approved a 50 percent tax abatement for twelve years on $3.3 million worth of improvements at a medical manufacturing facility. The abatement was on $2.3 million of real property and $977,000 of personal property.[38]

Is this enough lost money to protest? "Libraries and school boards often see the TIF glass as half-empty," noted John Laney, trustee of the Mid-Continent (Missouri) Public Library and former chairman of Kansas City's Economic Development Corporation.[39] He urged assessing each case on its merits, looking at the creation of wealth and jobs as well as the hit to public entity revenues.

However, sometimes the principle of the TIF, not the amount, demands action. For example, Mid-Continent and a local school district sought a restraining order when a homeowners association within the city of Lake Lotawana, not the city itself, established a TIF to pay for a new dam. Interestingly, most city officials were part of the homeowners association. The lawsuit argued that the city's taxpayers should pay for the dam. "It was not a major amount of money for us, under $50,000 annually," Laney said. "But it was a distortion of TIF that must be fought."[40]

"The concern is that any homeowners association could divert property tax to improve streets, curbs or things like that," added Mid-Continent's assistant director Steven V. Potter. For FY2007, that $50,000 would be about .001 percent of the library's $37.9 million operating budget.[41]

Benefiting from TIFs. But does the reverse apply? Can libraries benefit from TIFs?

Yes. Putting together a package of local and state tax abatements and credits can reduce costs for land, construction, and equipment. Utilizing several incentives could address historic preservation, environmental protection, and needed utilities. Creating a multirevenue package for your new or renovated library also plays very well in the media, showing that the director-board team knows how to take advantage of diverse funding sources.

The Kansas City (Missouri) Public Library provides one of the nation's best examples of using tax and other incentives. Its new Central Library, opened in 2004, was renovated and added on to a historic bank building in downtown Kansas City. The $50.2 million project provided 190,000 square feet and 500 parking spaces. Originally budgeted at $49,537,150, funding for the new Central Library included the following:

- Federal and state historic tax credits, $9,491,860
- Missouri Development Finance Board, $1,160,000
- Library participation, $11,700,000
- City of Kansas City, Missouri, $2,500,000
- Private support, $24,685,290

The Downtown Council, a group of city business leaders, formed a limited-liability corporation to buy and renovate the bank building, then leased it to the library.

One politically powerful outcome? Kansas City Public Library joined other central city libraries in Chicago, Denver, and Nashville by helping revitalize their downtown areas. Loft housing; retail business; restaurants; and comfortable, safe outdoor areas have taken root in areas near attractive central libraries. In Kansas City, it is called the Library District. Helping downtown redevelopment positions a public library to take a seat at its community decision-making table, discussed in chapter 5.[42]

Coping with TIFs

When it comes to tax abatements, some state library associations are on the case. The Michigan Library Association supported legislation to hold library millages harmless against tax abatement programs. Citing an estimated a $9.4 million loss in FY2000, it listed four tax abatement plans (also called enterprise zones) and five tax increment financing plans (also called tax capture plans) affecting Michigan libraries.

The Missouri Library Association's 2006 legislative program included monitoring "all legislation dealing with Tax Increment Financing (TIFs) . . . enterprise zones and tax abatements and the effects of the implementation of such legislation." It noted that public libraries and other affected districts may have to wait for fifteen or more years before a TIF or abatement is retired.[43]

The good news: TIF decisions are made by commissions whose composition and deliberations generally are specified in state or local law.

The bad news: Most library director-board teams rarely try to influence TIF abatement decisions. In fact, they could take several steps such as these:

1. *Ask for a library administrator or trustee to be named to the commission.* In Missouri, TIF commissions are composed of mayoral appointees in the affected geographic area. In addition, two members represent the affected school districts, two are from the affected counties, and one other person represents all other taxing districts, such as libraries, specific to the geographic area. A trustee of the Kansas City (Missouri) Public Library has been named to serve as the "other" person on the city's TIF commission.[44]
2. *Make sure an administrator or trustee attends each meeting.*
3. *Tell the commission that the library wants to be notified of any TIF that's being considered.*
4. *Assign an employee to monitor the commission's website for items such as upcoming meeting agendas, annual reports, and awards.* Brent Schondelmeyer, another trustee on Missouri's Mid-Continent Library board, urged monthly reports on TIF projects before city or county governments. He also suggested annual estimates of revenue lost to abatements or credits.[45]
5. *Have a library administrator weed through all possible TIFs for those deserving attention of the library's finance committee or director-board team.*
6. *Add more money to the operational budget for legal services should a lawsuit protesting a TIF be necessary.*

However, monitoring tax threats and even getting a library representative on the TIF commission may not help enough. Your library may want to consider other measures to increase revenue.

Impact Fees Target Newcomers

New rooftops mean more library customers. Happy Hollow's 1,750 new homes will justify a new branch library, but Don Developer got a ten-year tax abatement.

What to do? Consider impact fees. They tax only the new residents who cause additional usage, not current residents. Where permitted by state law, impact fees are used for capital expenses such as buildings and furnishings. However, the advent of General Accounting Standards Board Statement Number 34 (GASB 34) audit and accounting standards, discussed in chapter 1, indicates that library materials may be included. Most states specify that impact fees must be used to maintain standards such as volumes per capita.

Enacting a library impact fee requires an appropriate policy statement that is adopted by an appropriate local taxing authority. Sometimes the library board has that authority; sometimes it's the city or county.

Thomas J. Hennen listed libraries in Arizona, Colorado, Florida, Illinois, and Wisconsin that have adopted impact fees. His outline for a library impact fee statement includes specific rates, such as $450 for a three- to four-bedroom house; community and library profiles; the community's growth characteristics; a narrative showing what facilities are needed due to the expanding population; impact fee calculations; and municipal plans and code references.[46]

In summary, your director-board team doesn't have to wait passively for the next tax incentive to hit. Rather, you can campaign to get on TIF and other abatement-granting bodies. You can keep in constant communication with those bodies' staff and decision makers while monitoring discussions and decisions.

Perhaps most important, your team can start discussing how to use tax abatements to your own advantage. Get to know your local economic development authority folks; they know every tax break available. Working with them helps two ways. You position the library as a player in addressing community-wide priorities and may also enjoy major savings for that next new branch or major facility upgrade.

Advocacy That Protects or Gets Dollars

Since when is *advocacy* a four-letter word? You'd think it was, given how many trustees equate it to huckster-ism or selling used cars, especially when it involves local officials. "But nobody said I'd have to talk to the mayor," protested Trustee Trish.

In fact, the director-board team must talk to two groups, the people who use libraries and the people who fund them. It's essential that the fun-ders know your customers are also their constituents.

This guide defines *advocacy* two ways. One addresses shorter-term library concerns, the second its long-term role as a community leader; see chapter 3 for details.

The first definition: causing others to support your goal as their own. This type of advocacy tends to gravitate to intellectual freedom issues, discussed in chapter 2, and to financial issues, cov-ered in this section. Fortunately, as chapter 3 notes, help abounds for this type of library advocacy through the ALA, state libraries, and state library associations.[47]

Sidebar 4.2. Relationships Drive Oklahoma Library's Revenues and Advocacy

For the Eastern Oklahoma District Library System, a practical financial oversight process weaves together items including the following:

- Preliminary and final budgets reflecting county assessor and auditor data
- Advocacy for budgets by twelve city and six county trustees (eigh-teen trustees in all) with their appointing elected officials
- Proportional expenditures that reflect the tax revenue collected through a library tax in the county where the branch is located

What's the secret of success? An effective director-board team that assures diverse services to the 226,388 people served. The system has fifteen branches in six counties. "All of this takes understanding of roles and trust between the partners who carry out the responsibilities of managing and governing," said exec-utive director Marilyn Hinshaw. "The trust cannot be presumed—it must be earned by competency in tasks and relationships."[48]

Setting the levy. Historically, the district's levy has been increased only once, when voters doubled it in 1987. Individual county mill levies followed in the period from 1989 to 1995. All were successful.

Getting the money. All funds flow to the library from the six counties. They are due within one month after semiannual property tax pay-ments are due. While the library board has the power to sue in case of excessive county delays, it has been used only once, in the 1987 vote in the first county where the mill levy doubled.

The second definition: positioning the library to become a player in the community's power structure. "Players" help the library get a seat at the community's decision-making table. This type of advocacy is discussed in chapter 5.

This chapter emphasizes the first definition, specifically advocacy for funding. It is an essential part of every board's job, regardless of whether it has full or partial governing powers or is advisory. Sidebar 4.2 looks at a partial powers board. Sidebar 4.3 discusses an advisory board.

Despite libraryland's passion for advocacy, not enough voters or public officials understand why libraries need support. One national study by the Americans for Libraries Council and

Sidebar 4.2.
(continued)

Using board time wisely. The Eastern Oklahoma District Library System's financial management system blends board and executive director responsibilities. Each player carries out an essential part, with the director acting as maestro, a role discussed in detail in chapter 3.

Per Marilyn Hinshaw:

> The job of an administrator, as I see it, is to give the board the best possible means to keep up with their responsibilities, delivering simplified information so it is quickly and easily understood, and then advising on the potential next steps for the board. A manager must always have done the ultimate preparation, investigating options while not jumping ahead of the board to decide what is best. A good administrator must have digested and pulled out the theme of issues, putting it in clarified language, often using measurement for comparison so the board can meet its responsibility to govern.[49]

the Public Agenda showed that while libraries have high credibility in their communities, civic activists and voters are generally unaware of possible threats to library services. "Because most Americans believe libraries use tax resources wisely, libraries do not have to fight the 'cut the waste first' attitudes the public brings to so many issues of public funding."[50] It urged libraries to nurture this potential support and help translate it into action.

Relationships 'R' Us

It's simple. Effective advocacy, like the effective fund-raising discussed earlier in this chapter, is based on relationships. That means the library board-director team reaches out to the entire community. Why such a large scope? First, the library takes revenue from that community. Second, its collections, services, and programs reflect the community's diversity. Community relationships involve these people:

- *Local officials.* On the elected side, that includes the mayor, city council, county commissioners, and township commissioners. Appointed officials include the city manager, county administrator, regional executives, and appropriate department heads.
- *Business leaders.* Target your area's economic development council, chamber of commerce, downtown businesses.
- *Grassroots groups.* Maintain regular communications with civic, neighborhood, religious, fraternal, social, sports, and other groups.
- *Supporters.* Start with your Friends group and foundation board; also connect with historical supporters such as the Women's Federated Clubs.

Relationship management for effective advocacy starts with your strategic plan. Point out that the plan was created with widespread community participation. Use its vision, values, goals, and outcomes in board discussions to show why that new $1.7 million children's room is needed. Get ideas and input from stakeholders outside and within the library.

Sidebar 4.3.
Texan Advisory
Board Advocates
All around Town

In Texas, trustees of the Farmers Branch Manske Library may be found talking up the library in supermarkets as well as city council chambers or with the mayor. The library serves about 24,000 people in Dallas County.

"Working with our director, the advisory board takes advocating for our library very seriously," reported trustee Diane Graifemberg.[51] The nine trustees attend city council meetings, telephone city staff, and occasionally make presentations to city council about special requests.

For example, an economic slowdown in the early 2000s hurt revenues to the city, which operates on a pay-as-you-go plan. The board approached the city council, proposing a swap. The board would delay plans for a new central library to replace the current one if two conditions were met. First, renovations on the current building would be made quickly.

Spend extra time involving and informing your employees. For example, the Lawrence (Kansas) Public Library distributed a handout to employees concerning its proposed downtown replacement library. It urged employees to be positive and informed, while noting that no one would know it all. Key talking points addressed the need for a new library, why branches weren't being considered, likely location and costs, likely funding methods, and ways for staff to give input about the new library project.[54]

What's the single biggest hitch in relationship management? Procrastination. Potholes and leaky roofs dominate many board meetings. Can't advocacy hold on for another month or two? Not unless you want to stay in a reactive mode.

This section discusses using those advocacy relationships to fight two situations. First is an emergency: Your city or county attempts unilaterally to reduce board powers or budgets. The second situation covers using advocacy relationships over the long term to increase your library's public revenue.

Sidebar 4.3.
(continued)

Second, the city would guarantee that a new facility would be built in the next seven to ten years.

"The city agreed," Graifemberg continued, "and our building was renovated with new carpet, paint, and children's furniture."[52] Planning for a new library continues. The director has advised the board that in the very near future a consultant will be hired to begin the process.

Farmers Branch Manske Library benefits from an active Friends group that raises money for extras such as children's special activities and additional computers. "Our library is an important part of the city," Graifemberg concluded. "We are fortunate to have trustees, Friends and others who advocate continually for our library."[53]

City and County Attacks

For hospitals, "Code blue" means an emergency needing instant action. For libraries, local government attacks on board powers or budgets are "Code blue."

During economic hard times, library reserve funds and carryovers might look very attractive to hard-pressed mayors, city councils, or county commissions. Constituent complaints, say, about dirty magazines in the teen room, add fuel to this economic fire. The outcome? An assault on library legal powers and dollars.

Duels over Powers

Sometimes a local government is encouraged by professional associations. For example, the League of Kansas Municipalities advised cities that they had the authority to limit the library levy, saying that "library statutes are non-uniform and are subject to a charter ordinance. Thus, if the city deems it appropriate . . . it may . . . set up the library structure in a way that works for the city."[55] The Hays Public Library sought a legal opinion from attorney and state representative Mike O'Neal.

Not true, he opined. "To the extent a library board levies an amount not in excess of their established authority, a city, in my opinion, is powerless to reduce the levy by ordinance," O'Neal wrote.[56] The Kansas Library Trustee Association offered six steps should library boards experience attempts by their cities try to curb powers. Those steps included ongoing monitoring of city council agendas for ordinances aimed at the library, board members reminding elected officials of the library board's statutory powers, and attending every city council meeting.

In 2006, the Kansas attorney general issued an important opinion on county powers concerning libraries that likely also applies to cities and townships. It reconfirmed that per KSA 12-1220, "it is the library board—not the board of county commissioners—that establishes the amount of tax money needed to maintain the library."[57] Passing an ordinary resolution cannot cap library levies; the only way is through the home rule charter, which provides several points for libraries and their friends to participate.

Fighting Budget Cuts

Advocacy to restore budgets isn't for wimps. Winning the Super Bowl takes strategy, tactics, talent, and timing. It also takes stick-to-itiveness, month after month.

For these library examples to turn out right, it took constant advocacy by supporters, Friends, trustees, customers, and civic leaders.

Early in 2006, New York City rescinded midyear budget cuts to its three public library systems. For the Queens and Brooklyn systems, it meant $1.2 million each. For the New York Public Library, the impact was yet to be figured. Four months later, New York City mayor Michael Bloomberg made the three systems permanent line items in the city's annual budget. The FY2007 budget allowed the libraries to stay open at least five days per week.[58]

A massive 2004 budget deficit caused the Salinas, California, city council to order all libraries closed. There was a huge outcry in California and by the national library community. Over a year later, 61 percent of the voters approved a referendum that will provide an estimated $11 million annually for city services, including libraries.[59]

When Mayor Mildred or County Judge Jameel threatens to slash your library's budget, don't waste a moment. Get the fastest, cleanest start possible. The following steps tend to go from earlier to later, but could vary due to local circumstances.

First Steps

1. *Get help.* Don't struggle alone. Find out how strong the opposition's support, finances, and legal standing are. Within your state, contact sister libraries, your regional or cooperative library, and the state library. Get in touch with friendly officials, influentials, and leaders. On the national scene, contact the ALA's Advocacy Resource Center as well as peer libraries.
2. *Schedule an expert to review dos and don'ts with your board-director team.* He or she can help you be alert for national groups that have already piggybacked, or will piggyback, on your emergency for their own advantage; see chapter 2 for details. Ideal if done in person, a teleconference or videoconference works, too.
3. *Contact potential allies.* For example, if the emergency concerns TIF action by your city, talk to others who'll be hurt such as the school district, park district, and higher education units. Are they ready to

fight? Do they have the funds to help support a legal challenge? Will they help launch a public relations campaign?

4. *Notify the offending official or city council, mayor, county commission, or other body seeking the budget cut that the library will fight.* If applicable, be sure to say you'll have allies. The perpetrators of this emergency need to know getting their way isn't assured or going to be easy.

Clear the Decks

Set expectations among the major players such as the following:

- A steering committee will make needed decisions. Where possible, others will be consulted. But sometimes a few will decide what to do; others will hear about it later.
- It may be weeks or months before the situation is resolved.
- It will take many unscheduled hours of meetings, e-mails, teleconferences, phone calls.
- Fighting this emergency will cost money. The likely sources include current operational budgets, perhaps even requiring cuts in other areas; Friends; the library's foundation; and individual supporters. Don't be shy; ask for specific minimum amounts.

Steering Committee Tasks

Within the first forty-eight hours of deciding to fight the budget emergency, name your steering committee. In addition to the library director, likely library candidates are the board president, finance committee chair, public relations manager, and Friends or library foundation presidents. Pick one or two leaders from your allied groups, too.

Next, marshal your most effective forces for this situation. Sometimes it will be just one or two people. Does one of your trustees play golf with Judge Jameel? Other times you'll round up a large, diverse team of home-school moms, community activists, grassroots groups, and passionate library users to work with your trustees, Friends, foundation board, and director.

The steering committee tells allies specifically what they need to do, when. Don't make your Friends' board or school district superintendent guess. Provide the talking points they are to cover.

Communications

The court of public opinion requires sending a consistent message to customers, staff, and supporters. That means developing three or four talking points and at least one leave-behind fact sheet for in-person meetings. Those points must show how beneficiaries, who are also constituents, will be harmed by the proposed action. Tools to reach stakeholders include the media, the library's website and weblog, talk radio, speaking engagements, special events such informal "chat and cheese" talks, and more.

Will this skeleton process alone solve the budget crisis? Of course not; you'll need to add a lot of muscle to prevail. Once the crisis is over, don't let your hard-won advocacy expertise go to waste! Leverage it into long-term advocacy management that helps grow your budget.

Growing Public Dollar Revenues over Time

The second and final purpose of advocacy discussed in this chapter is a long-term campaign that raises tax and other public dollar revenues. For capital improvements, the goal might be remodeling a $6 million Carnegie facility or replacing 275 workstations and telecommunications. For the operational budget, the purpose could be adding sixteen full-time staff for longer weekend hours.

Whatever your long-term goal, show how it will benefit your stakeholders. How will the careers, education, and quality of life improve for families, seniors, homeschoolers, students of all ages, teen males, and others? When Sandy Soccer Mom and Tanesha Twenty-Something understand the project's benefits, they can make an informed decision about whether to support the extra taxes.

Open-Arms Advocacy Coalitions

Elected officials sit up when unexpectedly diverse, open-arms coalitions of constituents lobby in support of libraries. We are a salt-and-pepper team of a Midwest Caucausian and an East Coast African American and we feel very strongly about using open-arms advocacy coalitions that combine traditional and grassroots support. For more on the open-arms philosophy, see chapter 3.

Warning: Open-arms advocacy coalitions require authentic campaign planning. Don't treat grassroots groups as second-class citizens who should just follow a script. Instead, get timely input at several points. Hold early discussions between grassroots leaders and the steering committee. Together, critically examine everything, from concepts and outcomes to tactics and possible target dates.

After discussions are over, the library can massage them into a draft plan of attack. Then get coalition comments and revise it. The fingerprints of all participants would show in the final campaign plan.

Coalition Basics

Open-arms advocacy coalitions encompass much more than race and ethnicity. They also need to address age, income, gender, household size, education, and job types. Steps in establishing your coalition include these:

1. *Information.* Get data from your city or county economic development agency. Then turn to what is important to the grassroots groups. Identify their issues and needs, not just once but on a regular basis; for details on investigating local needs and values, see chapter 2.
2. *Benefits received.* Show how the library's proposed project will benefit grassroots groups in areas such as the following:

   - Job awareness, application, and skills
   - Reading and literacy for all ages
   - Personal topics of interest

- Obtaining tax and voter assistance
- Supporting students of all ages
- Free access to the Internet; library collections; and safe, attractive library facilities

That means telling the why, what, where, how, and cost of the library's proposed new building or fleet of computers.

3. *Traditional library supporters.* With all of this attention to grass-roots groups, weave in the other half of the open-arms coalition: traditional library users and supporters. Customers, donors, employees, unions, Friends, and the library's foundation all need information, too.

4. *Getting organized.* Start by applying the open-arms philosophy to your organization chart and selection of campaign leaders. Don't choose just Friends to lead. Instead, mix library and grassroots supporters for the top positions. Criteria for potential campaign leaders must include having both the time and the interest to participate effectively over many months.

5. *Funding.* Next, set up a Yes for Libraries committee as an IRS 501(c)3 organization to offer tax deductions to the limit allowed by law. Make sure it has a well-maintained database showing donors, amounts given, and when the hand-written thank you note was mailed.

6. *Databases.* Aside from donor lists, other major databases include voters in the past two or three local elections, past financial supporters of library causes, speakers' bureau opportunities, and 24/7 contact information for all campaign leaders.

One controversial database? Your cardholders. Is it a modern business practice or an invasion of privacy to send educational information to cardholders about that new branch or upgraded children's room? Technologically, it's doable. Computer systems could weed out minors by age; most would permit targeting cardholders in selected zip codes.

But while library technology would permit contacting cardholders, opinions vary. On the one hand, the ALA's advocacy handbook lists "library users" first of fourteen potential external target audiences, suggesting the desirability of contacting them.

On the other hand, deep concerns abound in the library community about threats to the confidentiality of patron information and data mining in a post-9/11 world. The ALA's Privacy Tool Kit provides guidelines for developing a library privacy policy, including notice and openness (telling users of their rights to privacy and confidentiality of their personally identifiable information), choice and consent (providing user options about how their personal information may be used), their own access to their information, and data integrity and security.[60]

Given the emotional, high-visibility factors surrounding using cardholder information, the director-board team should think very carefully about using it to send out advocacy information. While it might work for Visa or MasterCard, direct contact with library cardholders would likely be seen as an invasion of privacy in an era of many such incursions.

Galvanizing Grassroots Teams

Effective grassroots teams can make the difference for your Yes for Libraries campaign. Start with their leaders, then turn to the message.

Leadership. Recruit grassroots leaders to champion your cause. Balance an individual's interest and ability to serve with his or her clout with city or county officials. A call, voicemail, or e-mail takes only a few moments but may carry great weight. Criteria include these:

- Active in party, ward, or precinct politics
- A track record of working successfully with business or civic leaders
- Influential in regional or state politics

Help the grassroots leader make a decision about setting shared expectations. After all, this campaign may last for months or longer. It may be highly visible in the community and media, in part because the library is teaming up with new allies. Inevitably, there will be some differences of opinion about strategies and tactics.

Setting shared expectations about major items such as the campaign plan, organization chart, and leadership group helps reduce friction. Use a memo of record or other document to show the division of labor among campaign leaders, library supporters, and grassroots groups. Do include a calendar of events, especially who's responsible and the target date.

Once the leader has signed on, it's time to develop a grassroots message supporting the library's project.

Crafting the message. Decide on the umbrella concept or theme of the message—for example, basic literacy, economic development, formal learning support, and so on. Select the audience you want to influence with your message. Identify a perceived problem of the target audience. Craft the message to tell how the objectives of your proposed library project or existing programs can be the solution to the problem. Stating clearly how members of the targeted audience will benefit from the library's proposed project or existing programs makes the message relevant to members of the intended audience. It is also considered a rational appeal to the audience's self-interest. We illustrate this process in figure 4.2.

The message triangle identifies the problem (a social need that the library can help address), the solution to the problem (the library's objective), and relevance (why this issue is important to the decision maker). Then craft a short, pithy message for busy elected officials.

For example, assume the library project is establishing a family literacy program in each branch library. This could be the grassroots group's approach to Mayor Mavis:

- Theme: Family literacy.
- Problem: Children are entering school without preliteracy skills needed to succeed in school.

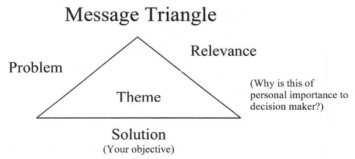

Message Triangle

Problem

Relevance

Theme

(Why is this of personal importance to decision maker?)

Solution
(Your objective)

Figure 4.2.   The Message Triangle

- Relevance: Mayor Mavis is on record as wanting to improve children's test scores.
- Solution: Offer reading support to parents of children from birth to age five.
- Message: "Adding three new staff members will enable the library system to help our children enter school ready to learn. Eventually, this will have a dramatic effect on test scores." A sports variation on that message might be "Three new staff members will coach families at story times for infants and toddlers. These children will reach the goal posts sooner because they will start school on the 50-yard line instead of the 20-yard line."

Provide statistics such as "There are X number of children under five in our community" and "Adding three full-time staffers will cover all thirteen branch libraries as well as the central library."

Wrap up with "Mayor Mavis, this family literacy program is important to your constituents because better test scores indicate better schools, which attract and retain families and employers. We need you to vote 'yes' for the library's upcoming budget that includes three new full-time employees for family literacy programs."[61]

Closure for This Round

Win or lose, have a party to recognize and thank your advocacy team for their help. Ask all grassroots leaders to make comments, along with the campaign's steering committee.

If you won, the first step is thanking the voters for their confidence. If approval was by city council or county commission vote, provide massive visibility with their constituents through steps such as photo ops, library appearances, and the library's website home page. If it's an election year, double your efforts so that constituents see how their elected official has their welfare in mind.

Be sure to thank all major participants in writing. That handwritten thank you note from your board president will help leave a positive memory about this campaign. Also publish a "thank you" advertisement in the local paper. Add the same information to your library website's home page. Naming the grassroots leaders and library supporters, including photos, shows how many allies the library has.

Also, consider supporting the "yes" voters in their next election campaign with your personal dollars and time.

Try again. If you lost this round, convene the steering committee to debrief on what went well, what didn't. Be sure to write down the major points, then revisit them in a few weeks when emotions have cooled down. Use those comments to consider ways to conduct the next round.

Talk with other libraries that lost, then came back successfully to win approval. Widen your contacts with and support from grassroots groups. At the right time, let the media know that this community need outweighs temporary setbacks; the library will keep pursuing this long-term project to benefit its stakeholders.

The Final Word

Protecting and growing revenue demands that every trustee, not just one or two, understands the factors impacting the library's revenue stream. Those factors include the following:

- Legal powers for library boards to approve levies and budgets
- Getting all possible types of public dollars available
- Understanding the legal curbs offered to citizens
- Combating and utilizing tax incentives offered by municipal and state governments
- Attracting private dollars
- Advocating to combat budget cuts and to secure major improvements
- Creating open-arms advocacy coalitions

Utilizing legal powers and effective advocacy do more than just get more revenue. They also position the director-board to become part of the community's decision-making group. The final chapter, 5, addresses how a public library can take its place at the leadership table.

CHAPTER CHECKUP:
"NEXT AGENDA ITEM: TAX ABATEMENT UPDATE"

As chair of your library's new finance committee, you're scheduled to give a board briefing on tax abatements next month. To speed things up, use figure 4.3.

Download the "Tax Abatement Checklist," which is partially illustrated in this figure, from this book's companion website to get going. Now you're ready for your board presentation.

Currently in Effect

Name/Location	Type TIF? credit?	Budget Operational? Special?	This FY $ lost	FY when expires
1.				
2.				

More . . .

Proposed and Likely to be Passed

Name/Location	Type TIF? credit?	Budget Operational? Special?	This FY $ lost	FY when expires
1.				
2.				

More . . .

Tax Abatements/Credits Our Library Might Utilize

Library project	Type TIF? credit?	Possible amount? project?	% of 1st FY savings?	FY when expires?
1.				
2.				

More . . .

Figure 4.3.   Chapter Checkup Tax Abatement Checklist

Notes

1. Based on items including National Center for Education Statistics, *Data File, Public Use: Public Library Survey Fiscal Year 2003,* June 2005, appendix L, "Frequencies and Distributions of Selected Variables on Public Library Date File," 75, http://nces.ed.gov/pubsearch/pubsinfo.asp?pubid=2005362; "NCLIS Study Shows $3.5-Billion Increase in Library Spending," *American Libraries* 36, no. 1 (January 2005): 33.

2. Denise M. Davis, *Funding Issues in U.S. Public Libraries, Fiscal Years 2003–2006,* American Library Association, March 10, 2006, www.ala.org/ala/ors/reports/FundingIssuesinUSPLs.pdf.

3. Based on items including "Matching Tax Funds with Allowable Expenses," a topic in the free Budgeting Basics Course for Illinois public libraries, http://learning.libraryu.org/home/, click "Courses," then select "Budgeting Basics"; Jim Minges, "Benefits for Librarians=Benefits for Library Service," *Loose Change* (March/April 2004): 3.

4. Rosanne Siemens, executive director, Kansas Library Association, e-mail to authors, June 6, 2006.

5. Mary Baykan, director, Washington County (Maryland) Public Library, e-mail to authors, August 21, 2006.

6. Based on items including Christine Hamilton-Pennell, *Public Library Standards: A Review of Standards and Guidelines for the 50 States of the U.S.,* April 2003, www.cosla.org/research/Public_Library_Standards_July03.doc, www.cde.state.co.us/cdelib/Standards/pdf/FinalCopy_WithCoverandAppendices_RevisedJuly11.pdf.

7. Based on items including "State Aid to Public Libraries," www.statelibrary.state.pa.us/libraries/cwp/view.asp?Q=40295&A=5; Norman Oder, "PA Budget Restores Funds for Libraries," March 15, 2006, www.libraryjournal.com/article/CA6314107.html.

8. Sara Laughlin, ed., *Library Networks in the New Millennium* (Chicago: Association of Specialized and Cooperative Library Agencies, 2000).

9. *Standards for Kansas Public Libraries 2006 Revision,* http://skyways.lib.ks.us/KSL/development/standards2006.html; *2007 System Plan* (Lawrence: Northeast Kansas Library System), 15.

10. Based on items including Institute of Museum and Library Services, www.imls.gov, search on "awarded library grants"; "E-Rate Funding Resumes," *American Libraries* 36, no. 1 (January 2005): 14.

11. "USDA Rural Development Joins City of Burns in Celebrating Completion of City Building Restoration," press release, May 8, 2006, www.rurdev.usda.gov/ks/2006%20Pages/050806-Burns%20Press%20Release.pdf.

12. "Bear Market Claws at Libraries' Funds," *American Libraries* 33, no. 8 (September 2002): 23.

13. Charr Skirvin, director, Plainfield-Guilford (Indiana) Public Library, e-mail to authors, June 16, 2006.

14. Lyn Hopper, director, Chestatee (Georgia) Regional Library System, e-mail to authors, July 13, 2006.

15. Oklahoma Department of Libraries, *Rules and Regulations for State Aid Grants to Public Libraries*, "C. Administration and Finance, item 4," www.odl.state .ok.us/servlibs/l-files/stateaid.htm#StateAidGrants.

16. "Library's Ebay Name Sale Fails," *American Libraries Online*, March 3, 2006, www.ala.org/al_onlineTemplate.cfm?Section=march2006ab&Template=/Content Management/ContentDisplay.cfm&ContentID=118748.

17. *Governance & Revenue Structures: New Field Data on Metropolitan Public Libraries. Analysis and Conclusions, 2004*, Chart 2 (Evanston, IL: Urban Libraries Council, 2004).

18. *Public Library Data Service Statistical Report 2005. Special Section: Finance Survey*, 18th ed. (Chicago: Public Library Association, 2005), 160.

19. Mary Baykan, director, Washington County (Maryland) Public Library, e-mail to authors, August 2, 2006.

20. Finance & Budget Committee Meeting Minutes, Kansas City (Missouri) Public Library Board of Trustees, August 30, 2005.

21. Based on items including Steve Coffman, "Saving Ourselves: Plural Funding for Public Libraries," *American Libraries* 35, no. 2 (February 2004): 37–39. The rebuttal was Thomas J. Hennen Jr., "Restore Our Destiny: Full—Not Plural—Funding," *American Libraries* 35, no. 8 (August 2004): 43–45.

22. *New Jersey Public Libraries: A Manual for Trustees*, rev. ed. (Trenton: New Jersey State Library, 2005), 39.

23. *Governance & Revenue Structures: New Field Data on Metropolitan Public Libraries. Analysis and Conclusions, 2004*, Chart 2 (Evanston, IL: Urban Libraries Council, 2004).

24. James Fish, director, Baltimore County Public Library, e-mails to authors, June 20, August 31, and December 4, 2006.

25. Based on items including *Governance & Revenue Structures: New Field Data on Metropolitan Public Libraries. Analysis and Conclusions, 2004* (Evanston, IL: Urban Libraries Council, 2004), 6; Crosby Kemper III, executive director, Kansas City (Missouri) Public Library, June 7, 2006, e-mail to authors.

26. George Needham, "Library Leadership Network Peer Panel, June 2006," as published in *The Library Leadership Commons*, www.libraryleadership.net/PeerPanel.asp.

27. Based on items including the ongoing column "Bringing in the Money," *Public Libraries*; Victoria Steele and Stephen D. Elder, *Becoming a Fundraiser: The Principles and Practice of Library Development*, 2nd ed. (Chicago: American Library Association, 2000); Andrew Richard Albanese, "Foundations for the Future," *Library Journal* 27, no. 8 (May 1, 2002): 40–43.

28. Based on items including *Fearless Fundraising for Nonprofit Boards* (Washington, DC: BoardSource, 2003); Carol Weisman, ed., *Secrets of Successful Fundraising* (Washington, DC: BoardSource, 2000); Kay Sprinkel Grace, *Beyond Fundraising* (Indianapolis: The Center on Philanthropy at Indiana University, 2005).

29. Based on items including "Frequently Asked Questions: What Is Cause-Related Marketing?" Foundation Center, http://fdncenter.org/getstarted/faqs/html/cause_marketing.html.

30. Jocelyn Daw, *Cause Marketing for Nonprofits: Partner for Purpose, Passion and Profits* (Hoboken, NJ: John Wiley & Sons, 2006), xxiii–xxxi.

31. Suzanne Walters, *Library Marketing That Works* (New York: Neal-Schuman, 2004), 186–87; Karen Bersche, "We're Selling More Than Wristbands—We're Selling Our Causes," *e-Glance*, January 14, 2005, www.alliancelibrarysystem.com/eglance/marketing.cfm?issue_date=1/14/2005.

32. Based on items including John J. Havens and Paul G. Schervish, "Why the $41 Trillion Wealth Transfer Estimate Is Still Valid," *Journal of Gift Planning* 7, no. 1 (March 2003): 11–50; Holly Hall, "Much-Anticipated Transfer of Wealth Has Yet to Materialize, Nonprofit Experts Say," *The Chronicle of Philanthropy* 18, no. 12 (April 6, 2006): 37–38; Peter Pearson, quoted in William R. Gordon, "Gifts That Speak Volumes," *American Libraries* 37, no. 1 (January 2006): 35; Susan E. Randolph, "The Promise of the Great American Wealth Transfer for Public Libraries," *Public Libraries* 44, no. 2 (March/April 2005): 93.

33. Stephanie K. Gerding, "Library Fund-Raising and Gift Policies," *Public Libraries* 44, no. 5 (September/October 2005): 274.

34. Faye Terry, public library services consultant, Indiana State Library, e-mail to authors, July 5, 2006.

35. Esteban G. Dalehite, John L. Mikesell, and C. Kurt Zorn, "Variation in Property Tax Abatement Programs Among States," *Economic Development Quarterly* 19, no. 2 (May 2005): 157–73.

36. Based on items including *Understanding Tax Abatement*, www.glpi.org/textfiles/Understanding Tax Abatement.doc; Tim Hoover, "House Advances Restrictions on TIF," *Kansas City Star*, March 3, 2006, C3(N).

37. Johnson County (Kansas) Library Budget, 2006, www.jocolibrary.org/index.asp?DisplayPageID=1994.

38. Sarita Chourey, "$3.3M Stryker Tax Abatement Gets Portage OK," *Kalamazoo Gazette*, June 28, 2006: 1–2.

39. John Laney, trustee, Mid-Continent (Missouri) Library, interview with authors, June 12, 2006.

40. Laney, interview.

41. Steven Potter, deputy director, Mid-Continent Library, e-mail to authors, July 19, 2006.

42. Based on items including Eric Adler, "Vision Turns a Bank into a Grand Library," *Kansas City Star*, January 4, 2004, A1, 12, 13(N); "Project Overview & Events Summary: Kansas City Public Library—The New Central Library," www.kclibrary.org/support/central/summary.cfm.

43. Based on Michigan Library Association, *Position Paper on Tax Abatement and Tax Capture Plans*, April 29, 2005, www.mla.lib.mi.us/files/ppctaxabatement200504.pdf; Missouri Library Association, *Legislative Agenda 2006*, http://molib.org/legislative/LegAgenda.pdf, "MLA will monitor all legislation dealing with Tax Increment Financing," 3.

44. Gary Carter, TIF program manager, Economic Development Corporation of Kansas City, Missouri, e-mails to authors, July 6 and 7, 2006.

45. Brent Schondelmeyer, trustee, Mid-Continent (Missouri) Library, e-mail to authors, July 9, 2006.

46. Thomas J. Hennen Jr., "Library Impact Fees," *Public Libraries* 44, no. 5 (May/June 2005): 169–75.

47. American Library Association, Advocacy Resource Center, www.ala.org/ala/issues/issuesadvocacy.htm.

48. Marilyn Hinshaw, executive director, Eastern Okalahoma District Library System, e-mail to authors, July 11, 2006.

49. Hinshaw, e-mail.

50. "Long Overdue: A Fresh Look at Public and Leadership Attitudes about Libraries in the 21st Century," Americans for Libraries Council, 2006, www.lff.org/long_overdue061306.html.

51. Diane Graifemberg, trustee, Farmers Branch Manske Library, Texas, e-mail to author, July 13, 2006.

52. Graifemberg, e-mail.

53. Graifemberg, e-mail.

54. "Tips for Talking about the New Library Project," Lawrence (Kansas) Public Library. Undated flyer.

55. Based on items including "Library Board Powers Attacked," *TrusteeTalk* 4, no. 3 (November 2003): 8, http://skyways.lib.ks.us/KLA/divisions/klta/shared/docs/trusteetalk/TT.Vol4.No3.pdf; "League Tries to Curb Library Boards," *TrusteeTalk* 4, no. 3 (November 2003): 3, http://skyways.lib.ks.us/KLA/divisions/klta/shared/docs/trusteetalk/TT.Vol4.No3.pdf.

56. Roger Carswell, "Director's Corner," *South East Kansas Library System Stacks of News* (November/December 2003): 1–2.

57. "AG Says Boards Control the Library Levy," *TrusteeTalk* 6, no. 4 (May 2006), http://skyways.lib.ks.us/KLA/divisions/klta/shared/docs/trusteetalk/TrusteeTalk Newsletter506.pdf.

58. Based on items including "New York City Mayor Makes Libraries Permanent Line-Item," *American Libraries Online*, June 30, 2006, www.ala.org/ala/alonline/currentnews/newsarchive/2006abc/june2006ab/newyorkbudget.htm; "New York City Rescinds Proposed Midyear Budget Cut," *American Libraries Online*, March 3, 2006, www.ala.org/ala/alonline/currentnews/newsarchive/2006abc/march2006ab/nycrescind.htm.

59. "American Library Association (AL) Compiles News Reports of Library Funding Impacts Nationwide," www.ala.org/template.cfm?section=library funding&template=/cfapps/pio/state.cfm&state=ca.

60. Based on the American Library Association's Privacy Tool Kit, www.ala.org/ala/oif/iftoolkits/toolkitsprivacy/privacy.htm; *Library Advocate's Handbook*, rev. 2nd ed. (Chicago: American Library Association, 2000), 9; Jennifer Burek Pierce, "The Scoop on Patron Privacy," *American Libraries* 36, no. 2 (February 2005): 30–32.

61. Based on a presentation in a Grassroots Library Advocacy workshop for the Georgia Council of Media Organizations, Athens, October 9–11, 2002, conducted by Ellen G. Miller and Patricia H. Fisher. The message was crafted based on material from Phillip Kotler, *Marketing Management: Analysis, Planning and Control*, 5th ed. (Englewood Cliffs, NJ: Prentice-Hall, Inc., 1984), 613–18. Message themes were based on library service responses from Sandra Nelson, *The New Planning for Results* (Chicago: American Library Association, 2001), 65.

CHAPTER 5

Getting on Your Community's Leadership Team

Quick View

So far, this guide has addressed four strategic issues. Two topics deal with the present—risk management (chapter 1) and local values (chapter 2). Two concern ongoing infrastructure needs—leadership and management (chapter 3) and funding (chapter 4).

The future takes center stage in this final chapter. But it's not the familiar world of library strategic plans, missions, or visions. Rather, this chapter addresses the director-board team becoming part of its community's leadership team.

"Hold on!" interrupted Director Donnalee. "Our team is nearly tapped out with business as usual. Why even think about economic development or community building?"

Because the library has two choices: Sit at the community's several decision-making tables or keep waiting underneath for crumbs to fall off. This chapter's goal is to energize your public library director-board team to position itself and the library as a power-structure partner, not a niche player.

This chapter covers the following topics:

- Many community tables
- The special case of economic development
- Positioning your library as a player
- Learning from others
- Chapter checkup: "Positioning Our Library"

As explained in the preface, check this book's companion website (www.pfisherassociates.com/scarecrowpress/sources.html) for additional sources.

Many Community Tables

Your community's quality of life and economic viability depend on several interlinked spheres. Each sphere, shown below, has its own decision-making table.

- Government
- Education
- Culture and entertainment
- Health and social services
- Religion
- Economic development

Getting a seat at these leadership tables means mastering the basics, starting with their goals, roles, resources, and authority. City, county, and township governmental levels require extra attention, since their legal powers, organization, funds, and processes affect every interlinked sphere.

Yes, it takes time to understand these spheres. But that knowledge is essential if your director-board seeks a seat at any of your community's decision-making tables.

Unfortunately, *seeks* is indeed the operative word. Because libraries are a tax-supported institution serving virtually all of these spheres, one might assume that most of the nation's 9,214 public libraries sit at some community decision-making tables.

Not so. In *A Place at the Table*, Kathleen de la Peña McCook examines the community-building literature and practice, noting the dearth of mentions about libraries in either support or leadership roles. "Libraries, like schools, are generally viewed as community services that are passive participants rather than proactive partners in broad visioning initiatives," she said.[1]

McCook discussed the comprehensive community initiative, a model that does capacity building through planning strategies such as those used by the United Way of America. She also showed how to link the Public Library Association's Planning for Results process with community building in areas such as arts and culture, city services and infrastructure, and employment and the workforce. Her suggestions to local libraries include implementing personnel policies that support community building through ongoing outreach by staff.[2]

Seats at Seattle's Tables

The Seattle Public Library uses McCook's model daily, stated city librarian Deborah L. Jacobs. "We are leaning toward making 'outreach'—as in *A Place at the Table*—part of regular performance expectations for all managers," she said. "Eventually it is our goal to make it a part of all employee work-plans since everyone has a role to play in making the library a key community player."[3] Jacobs believes in the library being in front of policy-makers, donors, businesses, nonprofits, and patrons. For example, the director of youth services sits on early learning and education boards such as the Mayor's Education Levy Committee.

Civic participation extends to the board and director, too. Each of the five trustees sits at different community tables. For example, the vice president of the library board is on the Washington governor's Early Learning Advisory Board and the larger Washington Learns education initiative. Jacobs sits on the Seattle Downtown Association's board as well as that of the Seattle Convention and Visitor's Bureau, among others.

Her advice to other director-board teams? "There is no future for the library without doing advocacy, participation, partnerships and collaborations," Jacobs stated. "Each community should understand that no table is truly set without the library being at it."[4]

Toronto Scans the Environment

In Canada, the Toronto Public Library has been engaged for years in a city-building process. Independently of the city, it completed an extensive environmental scan as part of its strategic planning. The plan identified four priority areas—books and culture, youth, at-risk neighborhoods, and newcomers—that complemented the city's priorities. "Because of the complementary agendas," said executive director Josephine Bryant, "it was easier for the library to develop and build relationships with both local politicians and bureaucrats. When the time came for teams and committees to be established, the library was an obvious partner for the City of Toronto to take on board."[5]

For example, at-risk neighborhoods benefit from the city's interdepartmental neighborhood action teams. Library staff not only helped plan the teams' goals but sat on the teams. And the citywide Children's Services Advisory Committee requested that the library be represented on it by a trustee.

Bryant stressed sound media relations for other libraries considering positioning for a seat at decision-making tables. "Good and frequent media coverage and attention help the public and local decision-makers understand the library's role," she noted. "In this regard the Toronto Public Library has been particularly successful."

Another must-do task is conducting a thorough environmental scan, including demographics, local economy, city planning, policy issues, and so on. "It is essential for libraries to know and understand the environment in which they operate," Bryant said.[6]

For many communities, that environment is dominated by economic development.

The Special Case of Economic Development

City fathers and mothers face intense pressures. For a library to become part of the power structure, it must understand those pressures. Of all of the interrelated spheres involved in community building, economic development is arguably one of the most important. Why? Both a growing tax base and local quality of life depend on it.

Jobs and Tax Base

Fortunately, business and civic leaders can get help from many economic development theories, workshops, and experts. For example, the Council on Competitiveness studied five examples of regional economic development—San Diego; Research Triangle, North Carolina; Atlanta; Pittsburgh; and Wichita. Its findings included the following:

- Economic development has just one goal: A high and rising standard of living, which can occur only in "a high-quality business environment that fosters innovation and rising productivity."[7]
- An area's innovative capacity underlies its competitiveness, which in turn is the foundation for its prosperity.
- Regional economic strength depends on factors such as having both local and stock-traded industries. Methods for formal and informal collaboration, such as a regional economic development corporation, must be available.
- Economic development takes time and must start with an assessment of regional performance.

National View

Looking at the United States as a whole, Council on Competitiveness president Deborah Wince-Smith stated that the United States "cannot compete on low wages, commodity products, standard services, and routine science and technology development."[8] What's needed? Success at being an innovation-driven economy that creates new value via steps including these:

1. Leadership in transforming industries and product segments, such as Apple's iPod
2. Leading-edge science and technology with diverse applications
3. Forming, managing, and revising global supply chains as well as delivery networks[9]

Your director-board team may not be conversant with business concepts in such reports. A crash course will help discussions with your local economic development corporation or chamber of commerce. For example, need to learn more about the "innovation-driven economy"? Googling that phrase gets over 90,000 sources. Googling a companion phrase, *new economy*, nets over 260 million hits.

Print sources help, too. One *Business Week* cover touted "Innovation Champions: The New Breed of Managers and Their Radical Cultures of Creativity."[10] Another cover was titled "The World's Most Innovative Companies";[11] one article urged hiring a CIO. No, not a chief information officer but instead a chief innovation officer. "Titles of this magnitude send a clear message to the organization: Innovation is an urgent priority and someone should be accountable for it," said Jena McGregor.[12]

However you do it, learning major business concepts facilitates communication with your local power structure.

Local View

Those leaders know that cities and local areas are the frontline in America's never-ending competitive war. So does the National League of Cities (NLC), which emphasized the national significance of promoting local economic vitality in its *Toward a New Economic Vitality*. Drawing on several NLC forums and studies, the paper's points included these:

- *High priority.* NLC's 2005 *State of America's Cities* survey found that 55 percent of city officials named economic vitality as a problem; 17 percent considered it a major problem, and 38 percent considered it a moderate problem.[13]
- *Competitiveness.* Speaking at an NLC forum, Joseph Cortright said, "The era of effortless superiority is over because other countries are becoming more competitive with the United States and their workers more skilled than they used to be."[14] The economy has largely shifted from goods produced (manufacturing) to services, especially knowledge services. Competitiveness means more than just costs. Instead, communities must show a high-quality labor pool, a desirable quality of life, and amenities. Cortright advised adopting a "first, best, or only" positioning strategy, showing what makes a community the uniquely correct choice.[15]

- *Workforce.* Economic vitality requires a skilled workforce. The report quoted former Federal Reserve Board chairman Alan Greenspan as saying, "Workers today must be equipped not simply with technical know-how but with the ability to create, analyze, and transform information and to interact effectively with others."[16] The report also noted that local leaders can make a difference "by engaging stakeholder groups and citizens in a process of developing an overarching economic strategy."[17]

Traditionally, that local economic strategy meant bringing in new businesses or industries. To compete effectively for that new headquarters, factory, or regional research lab, virtually all cities and other governmental units offer the tax incentives and abatements discussed in chapter 4. However, a newer theory promotes growing existing businesses.

"Economic Gardening"

Sharon and David Barrios point out that economic gardening "centers on the cultivation of local entrepreneurship [and] is more effective [than traditional business strategies], particularly with regard to long-term sustainability issues."[18] It favors local, small businesses, thereby keeping economic and political power in local hands. This in turn builds what Robert Putnam called "social capital," discussed in the last part of this chapter.

Economic gardening, once favored mostly by smaller, rural communities, now finds a home in large cities. For example, Sacramento's Economic Development Department hosted an Economic Development Strategy Focus Group whose recommendations included economic gardening to "grow our own businesses."[19] In New Mexico, Santa Fe Development, Inc., adopted the economic gardening model as the way to diversify the city's economy. The group's proposed plan stated, "By 'growing our own entrepreneurs' rather than hunting for businesses to 'come in and save us,' Santa Fe can become a more diverse and prosperous community."[20] Aspects of its plan included developing and promoting export firms and markets.

Providing an infrastructure that uses city resources wisely will allow for responsible, directed growth.

Listen up, director-board teams! Blue-chip national and local groups are calling for innovation, a skilled workforce, economic gardening, and more. They are also calling for local stakeholders to help the power structure land jobs.

Should libraries heed that call? Yes, for three huge reasons. First, those jobs mean a growing tax base, benefiting your library. Second, those jobs will help keep the next generation in town for years to come, building your community. And third, local entrepreneurs trying to start or grow their businesses need information to succeed. Information is your library's specialty.

In summary, economic development provides an outstanding opportunity for your director-board team to help community leaders achieve their goals concerning growth of jobs, tax base, and competitiveness.

Positioning Your Library as a Player

Like a fine wine, "positioning" has textures, body, and complexity as shown in this definition: "In marketing, positioning is the technique by which marketers try to create an image or identity in the minds of their target market for its product, brand, or organization. . . . Positioning is something (perception) that is done in the minds of the target market."[21]

The bad news? Most libraries do a terrible job creating a positive image with civic leaders.

The good news? Virtually all of the nation's 9,214 public libraries provide programs benefiting those leaders' constituents. Not incidentally, many of those beneficiaries—or their parents—are also voters.

If your library has programs supporting economic development, tell your civic leaders! The trick is remembering to cover all the bases. Describe those that indirectly help with jobs and the tax base as well as those that obviously do so.

Likely your library offers programs to families, seniors, homeschoolers, teens, hard-to-reach youth, the disabled, and other special populations. It may take years for story hours, foreign language materials, or the teen poetry club to produce the skills needed for your city's workforce. Yet those long-term programs indirectly help local economic development.

Education, Emergent Literacy, and Your Workforce

In most communities, funding for education is the biggest portion of the aggregate local budget. Not only is it costly, but education is a key factor in important personal decisions such as buying a home. People make decisions about where they live based in large part on the quality of the schools, usually determined by the test scores compared to average state or national scores. When public schools do poorly, many people home-school or put their kids in private schools to get high-quality instruction.

Libraries Target Birth to Age Five

The education landscape was carved up decades ago. Grades K–12 belong to schools. Higher education takes over after that.

But what about birth to age five? Since 2001, it has become the turf of many public libraries. A significant, research-based movement—termed *emergent literacy*—now links those libraries with parents of children under age five. Emergent literacy helps prepare those youngsters for school and reading.

Reading is essential to the knowledge-based economy. Unfortunately, studies showed that too many American school children were behind their age grade, especially those from lower economic levels. Sample research findings included the following:

- There is nearly a 90 percent probability that poor readers at the end of first grade will remain poor readers at the end of fourth grade.
- Knowing the alphabet letters when entering kindergarten is a strong predictor of reading ability in tenth grade.

Teaching Children to Read, a major report by the National Institute of Child Health and Human Development, prompted a partnership with the

Public Library Association (PLA) aimed at local libraries. The first steps in the partnership were to disseminate information about the report through all the public libraries; programs and publicity were also developed for libraries to use. These programs included story time for infants and toddlers and reading kits, with age-appropriate books and reading tips, for parents and caregivers to borrow. In a later step, the PLA worked with its fellow American Library Association (ALA) division, the Association of Library Services to Children, to develop a model program aimed at instructing parents and caregivers—"Every Child Ready to Read." It utilized the three developmental stages of reading readiness.

Both outputs and outcomes (see chapter 3) were measured in fourteen test library sites. Parents and caregivers evaluated the program for each of the three stages. The results showed that they learned new behaviors, helping them to be more effective "first teachers" with their children. Sample quotes from parent participants in "Every Child Ready to Read" workshops included these:

1. "I have increased talking to him. You know, we like bond. You know every time you talk to your child they kind of like smile. There's a bond there."
2. "I talk to him all the time. When we're going outside I'll say, 'What is that? Do you hear the bird?' He's only four months, so he just looks and smiles."
3. "It feels pretty natural to talk about the pictures. It was good to hear about the research so now I'm more definite in picture sharing."[22]

Libraries considering an emergent literacy program don't start at ground zero. They can choose from several materials developed by the PLA and its partners for the Every Child Ready to Read @ your library program. Its website lists printed materials, a speakers list of early literacy experts, brain development and early literacy materials, funding suggestions, partnerships and workshop resources.[23]

An Every Child Ready to Read Test Site

The Baltimore County Public Library in Maryland, serving a population of over 750,000 with sixteen branch libraries, was one of the fourteen test sites for Every Child Ready to Read @ your library. But the program didn't stop when the test was over. Instead, it grew.

Assistant library director Lynn Lockwood created a coalition of community agencies to support emergent literacy in the county. The coalition developed an action plan to enhance the well-being of children across the county. As its part of the action plan, the library put emergent literacy programs in many of its branches and in some nonlibrary settings. The library also created a new position, called early childhood coordinator, to manage the program. The library's efforts did not go unnoticed. Lockwood was awarded the Urban Libraries Council/SirsiDynix Urban Player award for her coalition building and the growth of the program.[24] And Baltimore County executive Jim Smith touts the program when he is asked what advice he would give to trustees and directors about becoming a part of their community's leadership team. "Many of our libraries have installed early childhood centers dedicated to helping parents prepare their children for school." Smith said. "This is a non-traditional but very important library service.... Libraries throughout Baltimore County have become true centers of community activity, and play a key role in the county's effort to put families first! Baltimore County is fortunate to have Jim Fish as the director of libraries for the county. Jim truly understands that it is a library's mission to reach out and become an integral part of the community."[25]

Based on research concerning how children learn, the Every Child Ready to Read @ your library and related initiatives by public libraries should help children enter school ready to learn. As a result, their test scores should go up as they progress through school.

Does your library offer an emergent literacy program? Tell your power structure. This long-term program will help your community build an even more competitive workforce.

Small Business Information Centers

Also tell those leaders about your library programs that directly support economic development. One widespread program offered by both large and smaller libraries is the small business information center.[26]

Cecil County (Maryland) Public Library

Serving a population of 85,200, the library's small business information center started with a $47,088 state grant that was matched with local in-kind contributions of $13,314. Since the grant's end in 2004, county commissioners have funded the center. Its website includes model business plans as well as links to licensing and code information.

Located in the central library, the center is staffed by a full-time librarian with both MLS and MBA degrees. The focus is on forming and sustaining ongoing relationships with business clients. An affiliated group, the Cecil Business Resource Partners, as well as local banks send would-be entrepreneurs to the library's center to get started.

Success begets success. The more the library directors, managers, and trustees are out in the field, the more they see possibilities for new linkages. The library attracted two other partners to the Cecil Business Resources Partners. One was SCORE, the Service Corps of Retired Executives; the other was BEPAC, Business and Education Partnership Advisory Council, an organization charged with preparing public school students for postgraduate employment. Winning a chamber of commerce award for small business support prompted invitations for the library to serve on important county committees.

All of these library successes helped Cecil County. Library director Denise Davis commented,

> We let people know about these successes. [We would advise other libraries to] make it clear that when you can help your county, you will do so. However, you can't always do what the county would like you to do since you don't want to drift too far from your library mission or vision. The risk is losing your own identity and purpose. But when you

can help and it makes sense to do so, really come through for them; in significant ways. Be a dedicated part of their team. In the process, be sure to get more and more parts of the county leadership to be part of your team.[27]

Chandler (Arizona) Public Library

Serving a population of 208,631, this library resides in an area known as "Silicon Desert." It is one of twenty-seven Arizona libraries participating in the statewide Economic Development Information Center (EDIC) initiative, which called for libraries to invest in print and electronic resources that would help local businesses and economic development practitioners.

However, the Chandler Public Library viewed its role in the state EDIC initiative as a passive one. It wanted to do more locally. It contacted Chandler's chamber of commerce and economic development department about possible collaboration and cosponsorship of a more active role in promoting the library's resources in support of economic development.

As a result, the three entities started the Local Engines of Economic Development (LEED) program, funded by a Library Services and Technology Act (LSTA) grant. One outcome was the Chandler Small Business Information Summit, an event that was a "one-stop" environment where small business operators and entrepreneurs could begin to understand the scope of available resources and compare them to their individual needs. The summit has become an annual event for resource providers to connect with small business operators. It also spawned a concept for business mentoring classes organized around the promotional theme "My Business Acceleration Plan (MBA)." The MBA plan was aimed at taking businesses to the next level; business-mentoring classes dealt with topics such as practical marketing and taxes.

The library's ever-growing involvement with the business community prompted these comments from branch manager Brenda Brown: "Make relationship building and networking a part of every day. Establish connections and explore commonalities. Remember the golden rule. Go out of your way to provide assistance and support for others. As a result, you will find that others are ready and willing to assist you when you need them."[28]

Public Library of Charlotte and Mecklenburg County, North Carolina

Serving a population of about 819,000, it has helped businesses since the 1940s. However, the Small Business Administration's (SBA) Business Resource Center was the primary resource for entrepreneurs until shortly after September 11, 2001, when the building it operated in was sold. Seeing an opportunity to be of service, the library proposed establishing a small business center at the main library. Funding from four entities—the city, the county, the SBA, and in-kind library contributions—resulted in the opening of the Small Business Information Center (SBIC) at the main library in 2002. Business librarians worked with clients, using print and electronic resources. Contractors with backgrounds in business and education were hired to counsel new entrepreneurs.

In March 2006, the SBIC moved from the main library to the main campus of the Central Piedmont Community College. A not-for-profit was formed—the BizHub Network (www.bizhub.org)—to continue the work of the SBIC.

The library remains a player in economic development in two ways. It has a seat at the table through the main library's senior manager serving as an officer on the BizHub Network board. And its librarians regularly work with people asking questions about starting and growing small businesses, assisting with research, demographic information, and so on. But, at some point in the development of the business plan, people are referred to the BizHub Network for additional counseling and development of their plans.

Senior library manager Susan Herzog advises libraries who want to be part of their community's team to "make sure library staff are involved in as many community agencies as possible. Attending Chamber of Commerce meetings and events, working with Boards of other non-profits, and being aware of what's going on in the community are very important. The library has to take this seriously and strive to demonstrate to people just how valuable the library is to the community."[29]

Leveraging Relationships

Small business assistance can provide direct entrée to business and civic leaders. But so can other library actions. Adding Bob Banker to your "Yes for the Library" bond issue committee or seeking chamber of commerce feedback during strategic planning gets attention.

That's because nothing beats firsthand experience. Business, elected, and civic leaders who work with trustees, the director, the Friends, or the library's foundation will form opinions. If the library folks are dependable, professional, and capable, their cause takes on added importance.

In California, the Pasadena Public Library knows how to get civic leaders on its team. In 2006, a citizen task force made up of banking, business, and civic leaders looked at the library's funding, as described in sidebar 5.1. Director Jan Sanders foresees the task force helping educate voters in a 2007 election.[30]

In Indiana, Carol Smyth McKey, director of the Morrisson-Reeves Library, was named to the Wayne County Economic Development Corporation board after seeking its input during the library's update of its strategic plan, noted in chapter 2. One joint program, WorkKeys, helps identify and train individuals for new or existing employers in the area. The program is conducted by the library, the Economic Development Corporation, and others.[31]

Sidebar 5.1. Civic Group Studies Supports Pasadena's Library Funding

When it comes to passions about libraries, few cities surpass the intense interest of folks in Pasadena, California. From the historic 1925 central library, designed by leading architect Myron Hunt, to the newest of nine branches, Pasadenans care about their libraries.

Third citizen group. In 2005, the advisory Pasadena Library Commission unanimously requested the city council to establish the third Future Library Funding Task Force. Its members included banking, financial, business, and civic leaders; some had served on earlier task forces.

The catalyst? The 2008 expiration of the parcel tax on single-family, multiple-unit residential, and commercial property. Tied to the consumer price index, its formula generates about $27–28 per year from a single-family parcel, totaling about $1.8 million per year for the library. Owners may apply for an exemption.

The job? Presenting recommendations to the city council on future funding for the library in September 2006.

Arguably one of the most successful libraries at leveraging relationships is the Chicago Public Library, which serves a very diverse population of 2.9 million. See sidebar 5.2.

Smaller libraries, listen up! You don't need to be as large as the Chicago Public Library to create and leverage relationships. The Aztec (New Mexico) Public Library, serving a population of about 8,000, also got the job done.[32]

UFOs (unidentified flying objects) might not appeal to everyone. However, they proved the catalyst for successful tourist attractions due to the creativity of Aztec (New Mexico) Public Library director Leanne Hathcock.

A local legend said that a UFO crashed in a nearby canyon—so why not take advantage of its notoriety and this unusual piece of local history? Hathcock suggested holding an annual Aztec UFO Symposium. Sponsors included the library's Friends, the New Mexico Department of Tourism, world-class UFO researchers and authors, and local businesses.

In 2006, the ninth annual Symposium attracted 300 attendees including science fiction cinema producers. It raised about $35,000 in cash and in-kind contributions. "The accumulated value of nine events is estimated to total close to one million dollars in publicity and awareness for the town,"[33] Hathcock said.

Sidebar 5.1. (continued)

Branches and their neighborhoods. Steps included reviewing community data. "We compared branch services with the latest demographic data by zip code and neighborhood," said director Jan Sanders. "Those demographic changes, coupled with the proposed closing of four public schools due to declining enrollment, will affect our branches. Where do we want to spend our 'work calories' in our facilities? We have to look at each branch."[34]

The task force also looked at the tax mix received by other libraries and the impact of the current library parcel tax.

Elections and advocacy. As of July 2006 it seemed likely that the task force would recommend a continuation of the current parcel tax and its formula with some possible "tweaking." If approved by the Pasadena City Council, that proposal would go to the voters in March 2007 for a multiyear extension. In that election, five of the nine city council members would be up for reelection.

"In the past, task force members advocated for the library parcel tax," Sanders noted. "We hope that some will do the same when this goes to the voters. Their support, along with that of our Friends of the Library group and foundation board, would be invaluable."[35]

What's the driving factor? Hathcock's desire to increase the library's gross receipts tax revenue, allowing it to pay off faster a $1.5 million debt for the new facility.

Library leaders sit at several Aztec decision-making tables. As library director, she attends the city administrator's meetings with department heads and also goes to city commission sessions. "Attending these meetings gives me an overview of what's happening in each department and how the library could play a role," she said. "It also lets me interact directly with elected officials regarding library issues and partnerships."[36]

Her trustees sit at decision-making tables, too. The board president is treasurer of the Downtown Main Street Association. The vice president is the chamber director. The board secretary is on the Aztec Trails and Open Spaces Committee.

The latest idea? A Committee for the Cultural Center. Hathcock chairs it. She brought in consultant Jim Connor to conduct an in-depth planning session with representatives from federal, local, and state governmental, business, educational, and service groups. The start-up group included National Park Service staff responsible for the Aztec Ruins National Monument and the Chaco Canyon National Historic Site; San Juan College East, Friends of the Library; the chamber of commerce; the Downtown Main Street Association; and the University of New

Sidebar 5.2. Chicago Public Library Helps Its City, Gets Support

Few public libraries find themselves lionized in a bestseller by national author Robert D. Putnam, author of *Bowling Alone*. But for the Chicago Public Library (CPL), this and other accolades aren't flattery—they reflect hard-won achievements. As the *2005 Annual Report* stated, CPL is "that special third place—beyond home and work—where people come to improve their lives, nourish their intellect or simply be entertained."[37]

Facts. In 2005, Chicago had 2.9 million population. That year, CPL's seventy-nine libraries provided 2.6 million free computer sessions on nearly 2,000 public access computers. Eighty-five thousand children participated in summer reading, TeenVolume, and BookAMania. The Chicago Public Library Foundation contributed $1.7 million (or 15 percent) of its $113 million revenues. Since Mayor Daley was first elected in 1999, fifty-two libraries have been renovated or built.

One major factor: Commissioner Mary A. Dempsey. The CPL has gained the unqualified support of Mayor Richard M. Daley as well as other civic and business leaders. Why? As its 2005 *Annual Report* says, the library "is at the forefront of providing innovative library services, technologies and tools Chicagoans need to achieve their personal goals and to establish our City's role as a competitive force in the global marketplace."[38] As a department head, Dempsey is a member of the mayor's cabinet, providing direct access to him. She also sees that the library has regular contacts with each of the city's fifty aldermen, especially through branch managers.

Mexico's LodeStar Astronomy Center based in Albuquerque. The Committee for the Cultural Center foresees projects such as these:

- A Science and Cultural Center featuring a digital planetarium
- A Community Technology Center that produces programs for the planetarium, with an emphasis on Four Corners Native American creation/star stories. It would also house a business incubation program.

Hathcock had several tips for smaller libraries thinking about getting a seat at their community's leadership tables. "Start with a community assessment so you can determine strengths and weaknesses. That will give you an idea of what organizations are already there and which are not," she said. "In so doing, you will identify existing organizations that might have similar purposes and agendas to partner with. Look for partnering potentials within your city and at the county level as well," she concluded. "Many opportunities lie just outside the city's boundaries in the neighboring communities. Keep an open mind and don't close the door to any potential relationships"[39]

Relationships versus Partnerships

One semantic clarification. So far, this discussion has been about relationships, connot-

Sidebar 5.2.
(continued)

Connecting with leaders. Chicago Public Library 2010, A *Vision for Our Future,* looked at strengths and opportunities. The four areas of strength were welcoming and safe physical infrastructure and presence in the community, current and diverse collections, dedicated and well-trained personnel, and innovative programming.

The three areas of new strategic opportunity are expanding and enhancing program and partnership opportunities; expanding information access, navigation, and education; and increasing usage and awareness of CPL offerings. As to increasing usage and awareness of CPL offerings, the report stated, "It is imperative that key decision makers, from the Mayor and City Council members to the Budget Director, corporate and philanthropic executives and individual donors clearly understand that the Chicago public Library is committed to quantifying and evaluating its successes, and continuously improving its collections, online information access, programs and services."[40] Note the three emphases: ongoing communications with civic leaders and donors, measuring outcomes, and commitment to continuous improvement.

"Public libraries must constantly and aggressively raise awareness with elected officials and taxpayers about the essential role that the public library plays in raising the quality of a city's life and in ensuring that the library plays an important role in that city's place in the global economy," Dempsey stated. "Constant communication about what the library is doing and why is essential if the library is to be invited to 'be at the table.'"[41]

Simply stated, the CPL connects people with their dreams, their neighborhoods, and the entire city. As a result, it has earned unparalleled financial and political support from the city's leaders.

ing a variety of long-term contacts between the library and diverse civic or business entities. They are likely to be informal. Usually the leaders are in regular communication.

However, libraries are much more familiar with partnerships, typically projects or shorter-term undertakings with both nonprofit and for-profit entities. Verbal agreements seem to predominate, although many do use written memos of understandings or contracts. One caveat applies, as McCook noted: "Although partnerships are a manifestation of two or more well-developed entities creating opportunities for collaboration . . . they also tend to represent collaboration at the level of administrator to administrator."[42] To overcome the fact that nonleaders tend to run library partnerships, you can still get needed visibility. Just show your power structure how their constituents benefit from the library's HomeworkHelper kiosk housed at the MegaMall.

Fortunately, advice abounds about library partnerships. For example, searching the ALA's website (www.ala.org) for "community partnerships" brings up over 2,500 documents. They cover a lot of territory, from early literacy to "one book, one community." They range from papers to press releases to notices of upcoming conference sessions.[43]

Another information source is WebJunction, a national cooperative of library staff sharing via online resources. Searching http://webjunction.org for "community partnerships" shows, among other results, over 120 documents and over 700 discussions (interactive message board conversations).

Yes, most of WebJunction's offerings currently target librarians, not trustees, but some topics are relevant to other aspects of board business, such as "Library Privacy and Confidentiality: Law and Policy."

Looking ahead, WebJunction executive director Marilyn Gell Mason sees an organized suite of courses specifically designed for trustees. One method might be for libraries to use tools developed by WebJunction. Or a template could be modified. "I can imagine, for instance, that we might offer a set of courses that cover national topics and then provide a template for libraries to make their own courses to meet local needs." A third method might be a blended learning approach similar to WebJunction's Spanish Language Outreach and Rural Sustainability projects. "We work with an expert to develop a curriculum and then work with a state library to train trainers."[44]

Yes, advice and tips help. But successful partnerships depend on careful local planning.

Partnership Prep

Think you're ready for a partnership with Mammoth Medical Center to pay for all family health books, magazines, multimedia, and databases? Have thorough director-board team discussions first.

1. *Purpose.* Why does the library want more partnerships—to reach out to non- or underserved populations? To get the attention of civic leaders or voters?
2. *Criteria for potential partnerships.* The partnership must fit the library's strategic plan and desired image. If Laura's Lingerie wants to sponsor a teen fashion show, you'd better think twice.
3. *Benefits to both parties.* For a partnership to endure, it must bring benefits to both sides. Remember, your special populations are their target markets. That's why GameBuzz, Inc., paid all costs for your very popular Spring Break Xbox Tournament—and has already signed up for next year.
4. *Formal policy.* Don't underestimate your board's differences of opinion about partnerships. It may take several board meetings to thrash out contentious points.

One thorny topic: How much library visibility the partner should get. Should it be signage on stacks? Home page thanks? A conspicuous "wall of library partners"? Small print in the library's annual report? Save time by checking peer libraries' policies. Just Google the library's name, then search for the policy of interest.

The outcome of your careful deliberation? A formal policy that defines how and where partnerships fit into the library's priorities. For example, the Johnson County (Kansas) Library has two policies that cover formal business relationships, including partnerships. Administrative

Regulation 50-30-25 covers the library's ability to enter independently into contracts with entities such as vendors.

Administrative Regulation 10-50-85 addresses program agreements with public agencies, not-for-profit organizations, and for-profit businesses to cosponsor a program or event. It specifies that any written agreement is to include items such as objectives, costs, who does what, and library requirements with respect to advertising or display of corporate or organizational logos.[45]

In Illinois, the Naperville Public Library asked local merchants to be partners, giving discounts to customers who also showed their library card. The Show Us Your Library Card, Naperville! program melded several national programs with its own goals. A solicitation letter, formal agreement, and program evaluation form for use by merchants were developed.[46]

Judging a Library by Its Friends

Partnerships can help position the library as a player with decision makers. When volunteers, especially civic influentials, spend precious time and dollars to help your Friends or foundation, your power structure sits up.

Running a library without a Friends group or a library foundation is like rowing a boat with one oar: hard! Not only do these support groups provide funds to the library, but they also show civic leaders that the library attracts committed, effective individuals.

One of the nation's most successful support groups is the Friends of the Saint Paul (Minnesota) Public Library. In 2005, it was cited for its support when the library won the National Award for Library Service from the Institute for Museum and Library Services. The group's vision is to "provide the necessary support to ensure that the Saint Paul Public Library is among the foremost library systems in the United States."[47]

The Saint Paul Friends routinely raise from $1.7 million to $2.4 million annually. Factors in its success include varied programs that attract donor support, including community outreach; a board, committee, and advisory group structure of over 100 people; and a highly formalized plan of action.

"We work with the library, the community, the mayor, the library board and city council in a carefully structured manner,"[48] said Friends president Peter Pearson. Steps include these:

- Regular meetings with the library director to find out the library's top funding needs.
- Convening an advocacy committee representing every city ward and every library branch to identify local needs.
- Advocating with the mayor that library requests be included in his budget proposal that goes to the city council as well as suggesting new items.
- Advocating with each city council member to support the library initiatives in the mayor's proposed budget. The Friends also lobby for new items. They went to the city council, supporting a library marketing and public relations position not in the mayor's budget. The council added it.
- Arranging for influentials to advocate with the city council on behalf of the library portions of the mayor's budget. "We involve highly respected individuals in the advocacy process," Pearson said. "Former elected officials are especially credible with our council."[49]

The Saint Paul Friends also use the power of matching funds. "If you're requesting that city council spends $100,000 on a library program, offer a matching $100,000 from your Friends group or foundation," Pearson urged. "City officials don't want to be criticized for ignoring extra dollars."[50]

Pearson's advice to others libraries? "Make your advocacy process formal, not off the cuff. Make sure you have a community involvement process." Working hand in hand with the library director is essential, as is getting influentials involved in testifying at city council budget hearings. Last and not least, "Never stop," he said. "We've used the same process for 14 years and it works."[51]

Partnerships and relationships help show the local power structure that the library is indeed a community player.

Learning from Others

It's a fact that not all director-board teams seek a seat at their community's decision-making tables. They have their hands full with necessary, repetitive tasks—making and monitoring budgets, evaluating the director, doing succession planning, and demonstrating accountability to stakeholders. Yes, their library may partner with Burt's Books for a summer reading program. It may have a strong relationship with Mayor Marlene. But for them, the cons of positioning strategies to join the power structure outweigh the pros.

However, other director-board teams see benefits in going to the next level by positioning themselves as players. Does that stretch their team's capability? Probably. But it offers one serendipitous opportunity: showing that their leadership attracts volunteers who raise money and advocate. Effective Friends groups and foundations prove that the library is a magnet for the able and the committed.

Jump-start discussion by your team of seeking a seat at your community's various tables. Review the case histories in this chapter. Discuss the following advice from library leaders.

Director's Visibility

A major challenge for administrators is securing the support of influential community leaders and others (power brokers) who wield power in your community. Connecting the library to the "powers-that-be" is absolutely necessary for public libraries to maximize their resources in today's local economies. It is easiest to get connected if library administrators are the ones reaching out. We can achieve this connectivity by initiating contact, being out there, supporting others, and becoming the face of our organization. Knowing one day we will need the power of well-known community leaders, we cannot sit idly by waiting for phone calls and e-mails.

We must initiate contact by being in the same circles and networks that the community leaders are in. Join local civic groups, volunteer to be a part of annual events. Go to local activities beyond those having to do with literacy. While at an event, don't stay in one place. Instead, introduce yourself to a few folks you don't know. You'll be seen by more people than would ever drop into your office during a six-month time period. Tell people who you are and what you do. Share your business card. Become the face of your library so when people see you, they think of the library.

You know you are successful when community leaders see you and either ask about the library or remember they have overdue items. Stay connected by following up on their requests. Doing so affirms that you value their request and that the library delivers needed information. The bottom line is that by networking yourself, you network the library and connect it with community leaders in ways that undoubtedly will be a good return of the investment of time and energy.[52]

Director Leads

The work of getting a place at the community table is really the responsibility of the library director. The board is the enabler and sponsor on behalf of their librarian. That does not mean that trustees cannot/should not have a seat at the table, but in my opinion, the director should be empowered to speak on behalf of the institution. Once afforded a seat, s/he has to feel that they are completely supported by the board of trustees. The quintessential job of the board of trustees is to make sure that they hire the right person for the job. The library director, as the chief spokesperson for the institution, should be one that trustees can feel proud of and have confidence in. Trustees do have a responsibility to help secure a place at the table for the director, but ultimately it is his or her responsibility to take advantage of the invitation, making sure that there will always be a future place at the table for the library.[53]

Nonusers Have Options

We live in a time when people of even modest resources have the ability to purchase books—in store, online or by downloading information. It allows them to by-pass libraries. Do not assume the world will beat a path to the library's door. Instead, demonstrate that you are family friendly and senior friendly, because these are the community leaders' constituents as well as potential voters."[54]

Get Leaders' Attention

Start by educating civic leaders. That means knowing each of their priorities and being able to talk about how library growth and development intersect with those priorities, such as economic development. Trustees can play an invaluable role in helping to educate the power structure, but that means going outside their comfort zone of just talking to friends. In every community where I have been director, I started a network by which trustees and the Friends board could reach every key community player within a few hours. A community's power structure includes business leaders, elected and appointed officials, civic leaders and the press. In different ways, they all affect the library through money, power and influence.[55]

The PLA is a very important resource for the nation's directors. Greta K. Southard, executive director, fielded two questions:

Question 1. Do you see any trends about directors taking steps to help their locality be more economically competitive? Reply: "I don't have any statistical data on this question. Anecdotally, I would say yes, libraries are becoming more proactive in working with community partners in showcasing the services the library offers that help create a competitive workplace."

Question 2. Aside from aiding economic development, what steps might local directors take to become part of their community's power structure? Reply:"Library directors need to work with their boards and staff so that everyone is telling the library's story. Library directors need to spend time creating and building external relationships with the organizations in their community—meeting and talking with the local government staffers, service organizations, chambers of commerce, etc."[56]

Social Capital and Libraries

The commonality among these leaders' ideas and advice? That community building is based on creating new social capital. In his best-selling *Bowling Alone*, author Robert Putnam offered this definition of social capital: "Whereas physical capital refers to physical objects and human capital refers to the properties of individuals, social capital refers to connections among individuals—social networks and the norms of reciprocity and trustworthiness that arise from them."[57]

In his follow-up volume, *Better Together: Restoring the American Community*, Putnam discussed how the Chicago Public Library, along with other groups, was building social capital. Reflecting on the case histories presented, he pondered the benefits, methods, and pitfalls involved with building social capital. The following points have been recast for a public library's director-board team.

1. *Recycling relationships.* Whether libraries partner with others to pass a bond issue or offer Hmong-language homework centers, the relationships built can be reused for the next joint effort. Using scarce time and dollars to build one coalition pays off when you approach those players the next time. Save time in the first place by utilizing existing networks and relationships for your new purpose.
2. *Leave no tool unused.* While the library-board team may be tempted to focus on the more familiar community spheres of education or health, remember that government policies and funds are essential to any of those spheres' success. "The argument sometimes heard that civil society alone can solve public issues if only the state would get out of the way is simply silly," Putnam said.[58]
3. *Bonding versus bridging.* Building relationships among like populations due to age, income, interests, and so on (bonding) is much easier than building them among disparate groups (bridging). Starting with an environmental scan, urged by several library lead-

ers as reported earlier in this chapter, helps your team understand community similarities and divisions.

4. *Stories help.* Talking to others about one's experiences helps build social capital. It's energizing to tell stories about ourselves, showing that at least the listener thinks we're important. "Telling and listening to stories creates empathy and helps people find the things they have in common, which then eases the formation of enduring groups and networks," Putnam stated.[59] The narrative-listener duo helps build social capital, helping both parties look forward to a future encounter. Swapping stories helps show commonalities, whether it's in a meeting or focus group. Inside the library, one example of using stories is asking job applicants to describe projects they've worked on. Their recollections, vocabulary, and insights add a living dimension to a resume or website. Discussing how libraries might use stories, Martha Hale notes that "stories can be used in three ways: to effectively introduce real people and real situations, to help newcomers build experience in an organization, and to discover and communicate knowledge."[60] Be patient! It takes months or years to build lasting relationships that can be recycled for different purposes. Given the turnover on library boards and in director positions, discuss adding community building as a value in your next strategic plan. It will provide guidance for your successors. "Building social capital is neither all-or-nothing nor once-and-for-all. It is incremental and cumulative," Putnam stated.[61] To keep burnout at bay, use milestones that demonstrate success and can be celebrated.

5. *Trust and confidence.* As people have successes while working with one another, confidence grows that they can do it again. They learn to trust one another to carry out tasks well and on time, as exemplified by the outstanding financial and advocacy results achieved by the Friends of the Saint Paul (Minnesota) Public Library. "Trust is a sociological breeder reactor," Putnam noted.[62]

6. *Recognize the risks of raising social capital, such as the following*:

- Greater polarization. Carefully discuss steps that could accentuate class and racial differences, as in building a new branch library and thereby accelerating the pace of gentrification. Not only are poorer people forced out of the neighborhood, but "when people are no longer poor, the idea of shared fate (and shared solutions) is less persuasive," he said.[63]
- Sustaining momentum. Beware burnout by key leaders and supporters, especially when initial goals have been met. Another critical point is leadership transition from the initial messianic stage and to an administrative one. A third potential problem crops up due to attracting new participants for whom the goal is not a cause but an amenity.

7. *Constant contact*. Creating social capital depends on ongoing, repetitive contacts among the participants. Libraries offer a unique site for that contact as a way of community building, as Putnam noted when saying, "The Chicago library system altered its fundamental mission (and changed its physical planning) precisely because leaders recognized the importance of shared space for community building."[64]

Positioning your library to get a seat at the power structure's table requires adopting the value of community building in several interrelated spheres. Among those spheres, this guide sees two of special importance: education and economic development.

High-quality education attracts newcomers to your community as well as preparing a competitive workforce. Economic development grows the tax base. Together, they assure an attractive quality of life and desirable jobs for your children and grandchildren. To the extent that the director-board team helps achieve those community priorities concerning economic development and education, it will have fulfilled its part of the social contract with taxpayers and donors. It will also have shown the power structure that the library is a proven community leader.

The Last Final Word

Director-board teams must take care of library business. Increasingly, that includes getting a seat at your community's decision-making tables. Doing so moves the library past being just a service bureau to being a player that helps achieve community goals.

Economic development and high-quality education rank high among those community goals. Most libraries support them in many ways, ranging from small business centers to emergent literacy programs.

Don't be timid! Position your library with your local power structure.

- Tell them how their constituents benefit from your programs.
- Get on the boards of the local chamber of commerce, economic development corporation, and key civic groups such as Rotary.
- Be named to your community's Vision 2030 strategic planning team.
- Broker initiatives that would help create jobs and increase the tax base.

These and other positioning steps will help your library become a player in setting and achieving community-wide goals. The outcome? As discussed in the afterword of this guide, "Going to the Next Level," your library will be seen as part of your local power structure.

CHAPTER CHECKUP:
"POSITIONING OUR LIBRARY"

You have been named chair of the board's new ad hoc Committee on Possible Positioning with Civic Leaders. Your first committee meeting is next week. To get things started, download the form illustrated in figure 5.1 from this book's companion website (www.pfisherassociates.com/scarecrowpress/sources.html); then fill it out.

Current Status
        Partnerships (Groups)   Relationships (Leaders)
Name   Goal/Purpose   Name   Goal/Purpose
1._____   _____   _____   _____
2._____   _____   _____   _____

More . . .

Top Three Community Tables Where Library Needs a Seat
Name   Library Programs That Benefit   Key Contact
                        Its Constituents
1._____   _____   _____

More . . .

Action Outline to Get at One of the Three Top Community Tables
        Dates   Positioning Steps
Start   Accomplished
____   ____   1._____
____   ____   2._____

More . . .

Figure 5.1.   Chapter Checkup Positioning Strategy Inventory

Notes

1 Kathleen de la Peña McCook, *A Place at the Table* (Chicago: American Library Association, 2000): 14.

2. McCook, *A Place at the Table*, 33–37, 101–5.

3. Deborah L. Jacobs, city librarian, Seattle Public Library, e-mail to authors, August 21–22, 2006.

4. Jacobs, e-mail.

5. Josephine Bryant, executive director, Toronto Public Library, e-mail to authors, August 22, 2006.

6. Bryant, e-mail.

7. Michael E. Porter, *Clusters of Innovation: Regional Foundations of U.S. Competitiveness* (Washington, DC: Council on Competitiveness, 2001), 9, www.compete.org/store/products.asp?cat=5.

8. Deborah Wince-Smith, "Out-Innovating: The New Competitiveness Imperative," *Opinion Editorial*, February 20, 2006, 2, www.innovateamerica.org/hot_topics/hot_topics.asp?id=67.

9. Wince-Smith, "Out-Innovating: The New Competitiveness Imperative," 2.

10. "Innovation Champions: The New Breed of Managers and Their Radical Cultures of Creativity," *Business Week*, no. 3989 (June 19, 2006): cover.

11. "The World's Most Innovative Companies," *Business Week*, no. 3981 (April 24, 2006): cover.

12. Jena McGregor, "Dawn of the Idea Czar," *Business Week*, no. 3979 (April 10, 2006): 58.

13. *Toward a New Economic Vitality*, draft (Washington, DC: National League of Cities, November 2005), 3, www.nlc.org/content/Files/E.VdraftNov05.pdf.

14. *Toward a New Economic Vitality*, 4.

15. *Toward a New Economic Vitality*, 7.

16. *Toward a New Economic Vitality*, 8.

17. *Toward a New Economic Vitality*, 9.

18. Sharon Barrios and David Barrios, "Reconsidering Economic Development: The Prospects for Economic Gardening," *Public Administration Quarterly* 28, no. 1 (Spring 2004): 72–73.

19. "Economic Development and Business Assistance Organizations Focus Group" (Sacramento: City of Sacramento, August 24, 2005), 5, www.cityof sacramento.org/econdev/msc/documents/Econ_StratFocusGroup2Notes.pdf.

20. *The Santa Fe Plan: The Cluster Approach to Economic Gardening* (Santa Fe, NM: Santa Fe Economic Development, Inc., 2005), 2–3, www.sfedi.org/.

21. "Positioning (Marketing)" *Wikipedia*, http://en.wikipedia.org/wiki/ Positioning_%28marketing%29.

22. "Every Child Ready to Read @ Your Library," www.ala.org/ala/alsc/ECRR/ projecthistory/pilotprojectevaluation/evaluationexcerpts/evalexcerpts.pdf.

23. "Every Child Ready to Read," www.ala.org/ala/alsc/ECRR/resourcesab/ Resources.htm, and www.ala.org/ala/alsc/ECRR/workshopsab/Workshops.htm.

24. Norman Oder, "Urban Player Award to BCPL's Lockwood," *Library Journal* 131, no. 8 (May 1, 2006): 24.

25. Jim Smith, Baltimore County executive, e-mail to authors, August 9, 2006.

26. Patricia H. Fisher, *The Public Library and Business Services* (Unpublished paper), 18–31.

27. Denise Davis, director, Cecil County (Maryland) Public Library, e-mail to authors, August 8, 2006.

28. Brenda Brown, branch manager, Chandler (Arizona) Public Library, e-mail to authors, August 8, 2006.

29. Susan Herzog, senior library manager, Main Library at Public Library of Charlotte and Mecklenburg County, North Carolina, e-mail to authors, August 28, 2006.

30. Jan Sanders, director, Pasadena (California) Public Library, e-mail to authors, July 27, 2006.

31. Carol Smyth McKey, director, Morrisson-Reeves Library, Richmond, Indiana, e-mail to authors, September 28, 2004.

32. Margaret Cheaseboro, "Aztec Librarian Generates Moneymaking Ideas," *Four Corners Business Journal* 14, no. 17 (July 31–August 6, 2006): 1, 2, 7; "Media Moguls to Attend Aztec UFO Symposium," FilmNewMexico Office, March 20, 2006, www.nmfilm.com/article.php?id=1145&title=Media+Moguls+to+Attend+Aztec+UFO+Sumposium.

33. Leanne Hathcock, director, Aztec (New Mexico) Public Library, e-mails to author, August 17 and August 26, 2006.

34. Sanders, e-mail.

35. Sanders, e-mail.

36. Hathcock, e-mail.

37. *Redefining Chicago's Public Library: Annual Report 2005*, www.chicagopublic library.org/pdf/anreport.pdf, 4. See also discussions of the Chicago Public Library in *The Engaged Library: Chicago Stories of Community Building* (Evanston, IL: Urban Libraries Council, 2005), 2–6; and Robert D. Putnam, "Branch Libraries: The Heartbeat of the Community," in *Better Together: Restoring the American Community* (New York: Simon & Schuster, 2003), 34–54.

38. *Redefining Chicago's Public Library*, www.chicagopubliclibrary.org/pdf/anreport.pdf, 2.

39. Hathcock, e-mail.

40. *Chicago Public Library 2010: A Vision for Our Future* (Chicago: Chicago Public Library, 2005), www.chicagopubliclibrary.org/pdf/anreport.pdf, 18.

41. Mary A. Dempsey, commissioner, Chicago Public Library, e-mails to authors, August 4 and 8, 2006.

42. McCook, *A Place at the Table*, 2.

43. Based on items including Mae L. Rodney, "Building Community Partnerships: The 'One Book, One Community' Experience," *C&RL News* 65, no. 3 (March 2004): 130–2; ALA Special Presidential Committee, "Information Literacy Community Partnerships Toolkit," http://irtstaff.austincc.edu/lnavarro/Community Partnerships/Toolkit.html.

44. Marilyn Gell Mason, executive director, WebJunction (http://webjunction.org), e-mails to authors, August 20, 2006.

45. Based on items including Johnson County (Kansas) Library, *Administrative Regulations 50-35-25, Contracts*; also *10-50-85, Program Agreements*; contact the county librarian via www.jocolibrary.org/.

46. Peggy L. Barry, "A Partnership Plan That Can Work for Any Library, Any Community," *Public Libraries* 45, no. 4 (July/August 2006): 47–53.

47. Friends of the Saint Paul Public Library, *Fulfilling Visions 2005 Annual Report*, www.thefriends.org/annual_report.htm.

48. Peter Pearson, e-mails to authors, August 23, 2006.

49. Pearson, e-mails.

50. Pearson, e-mails.

51. Pearson, e-mails.

52. Jos Holman, county librarian, Tippecanoe County (Indiana) Public Library, e-mail to authors, August 29, 2006.

53. Martín J. Gómez, president, Urban Libraries Council, e-mail to authors, August 25, 2006.

54. Jim Dodson, fund-raising consultant, Braren, Mulder, German Associates, Inc., e-mail to authors, August 14, 2006.

55. Mason, e-mails to author.

56. Greta K. Southard, executive director, Public Library Association, e-mail to authors, August 28, 2006.

57. Robert Putnam, *Bowling Alone: The Collapse and Revival of American Community* (New York: Simon & Schuster, 2000):19.

58. Robert Putnam, *Better Together: Restoring the American Community* (New York: Simon & Schuster, 2003): 273.

59. Putnam, *Better Together*, 283.

60. Martha L. Hale, "Stories in the Workplace," *Public Libraries* 42, no. 3 (May/June 2003): 166.

61. Putnam, *Better Together*, 286.

62. Putnam, *Better Together*, 289.

63. Putnam, *Better Together*, 289.

64. Putnam, *Better Together*, 291.

Afterword: Going to the Next Level

This guide discusses in an unvarnished fashion five strategic issues facing virtually every director-board team:

- Risk management
- Local values, the First Amendment, and challenges
- Leadership and management to achieve the library's vision
- Getting and growing the funding your library needs
- Getting a seat at your community's decision-making tables

Addressing these issues effectively shows two types of success—as an advocate for your library and as a player helping to set and achieve community-wide priorities. These achievements enable your library to carry out its part of the social contract—delivering services and programs that benefit four groups of stakeholders.

1. First comes the individual, the traditional library customer who uses resources from home or office or inside a library.
2. Second is the group, such as teens who read their works at the Library Poetry Café and entrepreneurs learning about business plans at the small business center.
3. Third is the community, which benefits from attractive facilities, access to worldwide information, and emergent literacy programs.

4. The final stakeholder group is the power structure, which sees a high return on investment of dollars spent on the library. Not only do its constituents benefit, but the library's pursuit of community priorities strengthens workforce capabilities, community building, and quality of life.

Libraries that meet the needs of these four stakeholder groups—and keep telling everyone of those achievements—take a giant step in assuring continued political, popular, and financial support. That support is essential in the face of economic ups and downs, competing organizations, and newcomers with their pricey ideas and initiatives.

We hope this guide's ideas and examples will help your public library's director-board team go to the next level by achieving two strategic goals: making a difference in your community and obtaining long-term political, popular, and financial support.

Index

About the Authors

Ellen G. Miller, BS, MSLS, is president of the Ellen Miller Group of Lenexa, Kansas. The company specializes in positioning strategies for complex public and for-profit organizations. Prior to starting her own company, Ellen wore all three library hats: staff member, Friend, and trustee. She is founding president of the 900-member Kansas Library Trustee Association and a member of the Kansas State Library Advisory Commission; she is past second vice president of the Association of Library Trustees and Advocates (ALTA); she was named to the ALA/ALTA National Advocacy Honor Roll in 2000; and she is a former trustee of the Johnson County (Kansas) Library.

She has conducted workshops for groups such as the Texas Library Association; the Missouri State Library; the Illinois Library Association; Solinet, Inc.; the Association for Library Trustees and Advocates; the Alabama Public Library Service; and the Indiana Library Federation. Miller has published articles in *American Libraries*, *Library Administration & Management*, *Texas Library Journal*, and *Public Libraries*.

Patricia H. Fisher, BS in sociology, MAS, MLS, is an independent marketing and public relations consultant. She has been a product manager with Verizon Communications for fifteen years in several business units— Consumer, Small Business, and Large Business. She has also worked as a research assistant on an Institute of Museum and Library Services (IMLS)-funded grant to study the supply and demand of subject specialists in academic and research libraries. Additionally, she has served libraries in a volunteer capacity for over fifteen years as a member, vice president, and president of the Board of Library Trustees for the Baltimore County Public Library; president of the Trustee Division of the Maryland Library

Association; member, committee chair, first vice president, and president of the Association of Library Trustees and Advocates (ALTA); and member of the Public Awareness committee, the Committee on Legislation, and the Core Values Task Force of the American Library Association (ALA).

She has conducted workshops and made presentations for groups such as the Maryland Library Association, the Division of Library and Development Services of the Maryland State Department of Education, ALTA, the Association of Library and Information Science Educators, the Black Caucus of the American Library Association, and others. Fisher is the coauthor of *Blueprint for Your Library Marketing Plan* (2006).